William Hepworth Dixon

History of two Queens

1. Catharine D'Aragon, 2. Anne Boleyn

William Hepworth Dixon

History of two Queens
1. Catharine D'Aragon, 2. Anne Boleyn

ISBN/EAN: 9783742869043

Manufactured in Europe, USA, Canada, Australia, Japa

Cover: Foto ©ninafisch / pixelio.de

Manufactured and distributed by brebook publishing software (www.brebook.com)

William Hepworth Dixon

History of two Queens

COLLECTION
OF
BRITISH AUTHORS

TAUCHNITZ EDITION.

VOL. 1321.

HISTORY OF TWO QUEENS BY W. H. DIXON.

VOL. II.

HISTORY OF TWO QUEENS.

I. CATHARINE OF ARAGON.
II. ANNE BOLEYN.

BY

WILLIAM HEPWORTH DIXON.

COPYRIGHT EDITION.

VOL. II.

LEIPZIG
BERNHARD TAUCHNITZ
1873.

CONTENTS

OF VOLUME II.

BOOK THE FIFTH.
CATHARINE AT GRANADA.
(CONTINUED.)

			Page
CHAPTER III.	At the Alhambra	. . . . . .	7
—	IV.	A Rose of York	13
—	V.	Invasion of Kent	20
—	VI.	An Impostor	30
—	VII.	The Child of Sin	40
—	VIII.	Fair Juana	46
—	IX.	Spanish Marriages	51

BOOK THE SIXTH.
PRINCESS OF WALES.

—	I.	Catalina	57
—	II.	King of Scots	63
—	III.	Richard the Fourth	71
—	IV.	More White Roses	77
—	V.	Clearing the Ground	82
—	VI.	A House of Woe	88
—	VII.	A veiled Infanta	96
—	VIII.	First Interview	102
—	IX.	Days of Courtship	108
—	X.	Bridals	115

CONTENTS OF VOLUME II.

BOOK THE SEVENTH.
ARTHUR AND CATHARINE.

			Page
CHAPTER	I.	Honeymoon	122
—	II.	Catharine's Plate	128
—	III.	To Ludlow	134
—	IV.	The Scots	141
—	V.	King of Scots	148
—	VI.	Margaret's Betrothal	155
—	VII.	Ludlow Castle	162
—	VIII.	At Greenwich	168

BOOK THE EIGHTH.
CATHARINE'S PARENTS.

—	I.	Toledo	173
—	II.	New Proposals	180
—	III.	Durham House	186
—	IV.	Estrada's Mission	191
—	V.	Isabel's Orders	198
—	VI.	A Spanish Comedy	204
—	VII.	A Change of Front	210

BOOK THE NINTH.
THE ENGLISH COURT.

—	I.	King and Queen	216
—	II.	Works of Mercy	220
—	III.	Elizabeth the Good	225

NOTES AND DOCUMENTS 230

BOOK THE FIFTH.

CATHARINE AT GRANADA.

(Continued.)

CHAPTER III.

At the Alhambra.

1493.

1. For years to come, with only now and then a break, the Princess Catharine was to live and grow in those secluded bowers where dark sultanas had been wont to make their home; a strong and fitful girl, more like her father in his pride of life, than like that Prince of Camelot whose mortal name she had begun to bear. Granada, as so many people had foreseen, was made the residence. The royal children had their rooms in the Alhambra; and although the holy war was at an end, the court had still the aspects of a convent and a camp.

2. A soldier who had donned the sack and cord, Alessandro Geraldino, was appointed to the post of Catharine's tutor. Born of a good family in Perugia, he and his brother, Antonio the poet,

had come to Spain in search of fortune. Isabel had noted these Italian brothers; seen that they had talent; and had placed them near herself. Antonio had become a proto-notary and diplomatic agent; Alessandro had been named cup-bearer to the Queen. Antonio had been sent to Rennes and other cities on her business; and in some of his journeys Alessandro had gone with him; but higher duties had been found for Alessandro in the royal tent. Mendoza favoured him, and on his taking orders, Isabel had named him tutor to her daughters, and especially to her youngest child. By one wise word, discreetly spoken, he had won immortal fame. When Queen and Cardinal were busy with the project of Columbus, men were much divided in opinion as to what the council should advise—the liberals wishing to support Columbus for the good of science, and the clericals opposing him as one who put no trust in holy Church. The clergy said the world was flat, and quoted Nicolas of Lyra and St. Augustine in their favour. How could priest and cardinal dispute the verdict of a saint? Mendoza turned to Alessandro:—"Cardinal," the Italian said, "though Nicolas of Lyra and St. Augustine are very good theologians, they are only poor geographers; for the Portuguese have lately been so far at sea that they have lost sight of the Polar star, and have seen the vault of heaven revolving round a southern star." Mendoza was convinced by Catharine's tutor, and Columbus had been suffered to annex an empire in the ocean to the many crowns of Spain.

3. In eating angel bread, in lisping endless prayers, in dancing with her ladies, and in talking with her teacher, Catharine was to grow into her teens. At times she went with her dueña to the bull-ring, beat her paper fan, and saw the horses gored to death. At other times she watched the smoke curl up beneath her lattice ledge. One day it darkened from a pile of burning books, next day it reddened from a pyre of burning men. She learned to dread the frown of an inquisitor. She saw the chief Dominican surrounded in the public street by guards who brushed the crowds aside, and seized offenders at his beck and nod. Her youth was nurtured in the sentiment of a war of race and creed. In hall and tower she met the gaze of captive damsels, who had yielded on a pledge of mercy, which her mother had not deigned to keep. She could not close her ear on tales of Jews being burnt, and Moors being sold for slaves; for such events were called by those about her court the highest glory of her mother's reign.

4. Yet, in the beauty of their home, and in the landscapes which surround that home, there lay a means of education for the royal children better than the monks and friars could give. They lived with nature, and they fed on art. Of all the structures which adorned this earth, the home of Catharine stood the first in physical beauty. To her right and left, the eye ran out on gracious lines. Below the tower of the Comares, on the pole of which a cross had now replaced the crescent, spread a scene that an Arabian poet had extolled beyond the

valley of Damascus. Here the snow-line of the great sierras gave a hint of Lebanon. There the vega flowed through orchards, vineyards, gardens all but tropical in form and tint. The courts and alleys at her feet were perfect. As she strolled about the labyrinths of her palace, she could catch the jet and flash of fountains; peep from the purple gloom of Abd-allah's hall into the fiery noon-tide of the Court of Lions; breathe her evening hymn from the ventana of Zoraya; look into the dark ravines, made musical in their leafy shadows by the Darro; train her vine-shoots through the fretwork of innumerable balconies; reach at orange and pomegranate, as the fruit hung burning from her garden wall; and in the moments when a rarer spirit touched her fancy, she could dally with the secrets of the Moorish arch, and catch a meaning in those arabesques which clothed her walls with services of prayer and praise.

5. The Queen, her mother, seemed to love the Alhambra better than her palace in Toledo and her Castle on the Mount. She built a row of sheds within the garden for her brethren, the Franciscans, in whose chapel she proposed to lay her dust. Granada was her trophy, and the people of Granada had no public rights. As ruler of the Caliphate she was free from charter, privilege, and fundamental pact. But she was conscious that her conquest must be held as it was won—by sleepless watch and curb of military force. Though bridled, an inflammable people filled the streets and squares. The roughs who had so often stormed the palace

might renew their riot; and beyond the ridge, now called the Last Sigh of the Moor, a mountain tract extended towards the sea, in which an active and despairing remnant of the Moslems stood entrenched. The princes of Granada, owners of the palaces beneath her eyes, had locked their doors and carried off their keys, believing that a time must come when the Compassionate would relent Him of his anger, and the Moslem chivalry would swarm once more through the vermilion gates. The victors had to watch and pray; to keep such watch as steels the nerve, to breathe such prayer as sears and numbs the heart.

6. In such a school the girl could learn but little of that world in which on marrying she would have to live. King Henry wished her to be taught a little French; the language of his court and household; but her Spanish and Italian tutors could not teach her French. The brethren of St. Dominic hated France; for French theology, as taught at Paris, was a liberal science, which those brethren called the froth of hell. Nor were the brethren of St. Francis gracious towards the French. A friar of Toledo looked upon his brother of the Sorbonne as a lewd and tipsy fool. All liberal thought and liberal speech were banished from the court. To thrum a lute, to sing a ballad, to recite a prayer, to work an altar-cloth, were safe and useful things, and Catharine's sisters, when they passed into the world as queens and duchesses, knew but little else. A woman of her country had no call to be a learned clerk. Her duty was to find a good confessor, and

commit her soul to him. He was to answer for her. When she gave her soul to him, as she might give her body to a leech, she had no more to do than follow his advice, and leave the burden in his arms. "Confess to a man," wrote Fray Andreas to her sister, "who keeps his rule, who has not a pin of his own, and to whom your highness can give nothing, and show no favour—only to the convent in which he lives." A good confessor for a princess must be an observant friar. "He only," added Fray Andreas, "can give a good account of your soul to God." But if Catharine knew but little of the world, she knew still less of the mysterious isle in which her lot was cast. She never saw an English face; she rarely heard an English word. Prince Arthur was to her a name, a shade, a dream. Her right to bear his title was in doubt. The ladies of her household gave her many titles: Doña Catalina, Señora Infanta, Señora of Spain, Princess of England, Princess of Wales: but no one title seemed her own beyond the rest. Her sisters were engaged and disengaged as war and peace decided Spain to seek alliances with Austria, Portugal, or France. Even Padre Alessandro could not tell his pupil to what country she might have to go as queen; or, if she went to England, of what monarch she might have to be the bride.

CHAPTER IV.

A Rose of York.

1493-4.

1. GRANADA being secured, the King rode up to Barcelona, where the state of public feeling, and the treaty of the Pyrenees, required his instant care. A crazy patriot, Juan de Cañamares, took upon himself the mission of revenge, and stabbed the King in open day. This crime restored Fernando to a share of public favour. Many of the grandees of his kingdom rode to pay him court; the cities hastened to denounce the regicide; and for a season both the King and Queen enjoyed some breath of popular applause. A little softened by his pain and by the public cheer, Fernando rode to Zaragoza, where, in his ancestral home, the Aljaferia, surrounded by his knights and nobles, he proposed to rest until his wound should heal.

2. While Isabel was nursing him at Barcelona, she received a letter from a man whose signature was that of Richard, Duke of York. This letter, well conceived and finely penned, implored the Queen to lend the writer help in the recovery of his crown. He told her, briefly, that his brother Edward, King of England, had been murdered in the Tower; that he himself had been delivered to

a ruffian to be killed; that the assassins, having pity on his youth, had spared his life; that they had sworn him on the bread and wine to keep the secret of his birth; that they had sent him over sea in company of two warders, who had hidden him in Portugal; and that, on hearing how his uncle, Gloucester, had been slain in battle, he had sailed for Cork, where he had instantly been recognised as Edward's son. What followed, as he told the Queen his story, had been no less striking than these opening scenes. Ormonde and Kildare, his kinsmen, had received him as a prince. The King of France had asked him to his court, and after testing him by many proofs, had offered to assist him with a fleet and army to regain his father's crown. But since the King made peace with the usurper, the Duke of York had ceased to lean on France, though Charles was still his brother and his friend. On quitting Paris he had gone to Mechlin, where his aunt, the Duchess Margaret, held her court. The Duchess took him to her heart, and certified his royal birth. The Emperor had recognised him as King Edward's son. Philip, Archduke of Austria, Frederick, Duke of Saxony, Hans, King of Denmark, and James, King of Scots, all recognised in him King Edward's son. The King of Scots had taken up his cause, and many of the English lords were only waiting for a sign to rise in his behalf. Since Isabel was of his blood, and was a just and pious queen, he prayed her to have pity on his youth, to plead his misery with Fernando, and to aid him in his contest with that Earl of Richmond who had seized his lawful crown. The writer was prepared to offer, in return for help, a true and faithful treaty with the King and Queen of Spain.

3. The writer of this letter was a youth of noble presence and accomplishments; so like King Edward that his face was "as a magnet to the partizans of York." Two tales were told of him while he was yet alive; and Henry, somewhat early in his venture, gave his countenance to the first of these imaginary tales. In this account, the youth is born in Tournai, on the river Scheldt; a Fleming, one of Duchess Margaret's subjects; son of Hans Osbek, a petty officer in the town. His folk are bailiffs, watermen, collectors, and the like; all poor and needy people, struggling for their daily crust. His name is Peter, which the neighbours change to Peterkin and Perkin. Though a lad of lowly birth, he hopes to make a figure; so he drops by boat to Antwerp, and from Antwerp sails by ship to London, and in London lives as servant to a Jew. This Jew, a convert from his faith, is known to Edward the Fourth, who is good enough to stand his sponsor, and bestow on him his royal name. Here Perkin sees the King, and has the means of catching all those tricks of eye and tones of voice which afterwards make the partizans of York declare him to be Edward's son. He sails for Portugal, where he serves a one-eyed knight, until he leaves with Pregent Menou, a Breton trader, who conveys him into Ireland, where he first declares himself to Walters, Mayor of Cork.

4. A second story was invented later on, in order to account for facts which Henry's story leaves untouched. This second tale is French in origin, and is sustained by documents under Charles's royal seal. According to this French report, the Duke of York is born a Portuguese. His father is a barber, carrying on his trade in Lisbon; and the man called Perkin Warbeck is that barber's boy. The youth has wandered up and down the world, and picked up many arts and tongues. He is a clever lad, but cannot cheat a parent's eyes. The Lisbon barber is alive, and willing to appear against his son. The barber's wife is also living, and is ready to denounce her child. These facts, the French declare, have been investigated by the king-at-arms in Lisbon, and the King of France is ready to produce his proofs—if only Henry, in return, will give up Spain and act in concert with the French. How any Lisbon barber came to bear the name of Warbeck is not mentioned in this French account.

5. A third and merrier story lightens modern books; a story penned by Bacon in a mood that would have made Fernando laugh and Henry swear. In Bacon's romance, Perkin is a sort of Ariel, who can float and fly, and daze men's eyes by magic arts; a youth of such "fine shape and form," and of such "crafty and bewitching fashion," that he acts like "a kind of fascination and enchantment to those who saw and heard him." Perkin is the son of Osbek, but this Osbek is himself the Jew. A pretty wife—as fair as Mistress Shore—entices Edward to her husband's house. She bears a son,

and Edward the Fourth is sponsor to the child. Her boy is christened Peter, which is afterwards corrupted into Perkin. Jests are made about the pretty Jewess and the merry King. The child is called King Edward's god-son, and in sport King Edward's son. These jests and sports take form in Peter's brain. He shapes the plan of an imposture. Bacon thinks he may have been King Edward's offspring by the pretty Jewess, and would thus account for a resemblance which the hottest enemies of the youth could not deny.

6. This romance, which arose from some mistakes of name and place, was just as true as Charles's tale. One man could tell the truth. Were both the princes slain by Tyrrell and his comrades? Tyrrell was alive. How had this murderer of his prince escaped the gallows? He had got a pardon from the Duke of Gloucester! Henry was not slow to execute the law on other sinners who could plead a pardon by the fallen prince. Was Tyrrell master of some secret which the Tudor king was forced to buy? Instead of hanging Tyrrell, Henry had promoted him to offices of trust. The regicide was a knight of the King's body, and enriched by many a royal gift. Henry had made Tyrrell Sheriff of Glamorganshire for life, Chancellor of that shire for life, and Steward of that shire for life. Henry had made him Captain of the fort at Guisnes; had made him Constable of Cardiff Castle; had given him the appointment of Chief Forester of a county, with the power of naming all the coroners and clerks. Why was this murderer taken into so much grace? Guisnes

was an important post, and Cardiff also an important post. Had he a tale to tell which Henry feared to hear? A second man could also tell the truth. Where was that Breton trader, Pregent Menou, who had brought the prince from Portugal to Cork? If not in Henry's closet, he was certainly within his reach. Was he invited to reveal the facts within his knowledge? Was he brought before a magistrate and asked to state the details of his life on oath? Not once. Instead of being induced to speak, Menou was silenced by the King, and when the time for his reward had come, the man was paid in money and a place of trust.

7. When Isabel received that letter from the Duke of York, she thought his story true. She had some means of testing him, especially on his life in Portugal; and nothing to be learnt in Lisbon tended to produce a change of mind. Among the papers at Simancas, which were once the secrets of her closet, is a key to certain Latin numerals used by her and by her husband in their cyphers. Every royal person has a number to his name. The Pope, the Emperor, the Kings of France and England, have their numbers; each in order of his rank, as he was measured in the court of Spain. The Duchess Margaret has a number, and Ferdinando, King of Naples, has a number. None but royal persons have a number in this key. A note explains that other persons of distinction, not of reigning houses, are included in a second key. Among the royal names is that of Richard, Duke of York; his place between Duchess Margaret, his aunt, and Ferdi-

nando, King of Naples. Such a record is decisive. Let the youth who signed that name be either Osbek, Warbeck, or Plantagenet, the King and Queen then living in the Aljaferia thought he was King Edward's son.

8. Yet Isabel, to whom this letter opened an abyss, was slow to pledge herself. If Richard, Duke of York, should get his own, he would require a wife; and Catharine, her youngest daughter, must be queen, whoever was the English king. But Richard had not tried his strength, as yet; and till he proved his mettle she must keep herself unpledged. She therefore wrote a note to Duchess Margaret (meant for Richard's eye), expressing all the feelings of her heart towards the unhappy prince, and offering him, as one of her own blood, the tenderest friendship and the best support.

CHAPTER V.

Invasion of Kent.

1495.

1. THREE years the titular Duke of York had lived in royal courts; the court of Charles, the court of Margaret, the court of Max; and neither in his speech and gait, nor in his family affairs, had he betrayed himself. If he were acting, men had never seen an actor like him since the world began. A mayor of Cork, like Walters, might be fooled by tricks of speech, but Max and Charles were born in purple, and could hardly be misled by a comedian. Max and Charles had means of finding out, and having much to gain or lose through him, they are not likely to have left these means untried. The young man lived in Margaret's house. She was his aunt, and she had seen him in his youth. Yet Margaret never varied in her strong conviction that he was her brother's son. It may be true, as Henry's scribes gave out, that she disliked the English King and wished to cast him out; but if a base pretender were to gain the crown, she would be also casting out the line of York—her niece the reigning Queen; her other nieces, sisters of that reigning Queen; her nephew, Edward Plantagenet; her nephew, Edmond de la Pole; her

daughter's children, Philip and Marguerite; and, last of all, herself. She could not aid a counterfeit duke without deposing all her kith and kin. Unless it can be shown that Margaret was insane, she must be taken as a witness to the fact. If Margaret knew the man as an impostor, she was doing her utmost to unseat her niece, to set aside her nephews, and to dispossess the house of York, in order that a rogue, a peasant, and a stranger, might enjoy her brother's throne. If she was not an honest witness she was nothing but a crazy fool. What fact in her career permits a man of sense to brand her as a crazy fool? In writing to the Pope, she dwelt on her affinity with Richard, Duke of York. He was her brother's son, her nephew, and her liege. His face, his voice, were evidence to her eyes and ears. She could not be mistaken, she declared, in one who stood so near to her in blood.

2. A dozen princes saw him, spoke with him, and judged him; from the crafty Charles of France to the chivalrous James of Scotland; yet in every court of Europe his appearance and his story were approved. Fine ladies listened to his talk, and found in every sentence from his lips a secret charm. Soft, winsome, witty, he engaged all hearts. The mayor of Cork no sooner saw his face than he became a convert to his cause for life and death. Kildare and Desmond were not louder in his praise than artizans and kernes. A sort of royal gift he had; a grace to work on kings and princes even more than on the common herd of men. The Archduke Philip loved him as an elder brother. Max

regarded his affairs as more important than the business of his empire. Though a Diet was proclaimed, and though a hundred princes, dukes, and cardinals were assembling, Max could find no time to meet them. "Richard, King of England," was, he said, "about to sail," and Max being busy with that great event, his princes, dukes, and cardinals must wait.

3. Ten years ago, two thousand men had sailed from Normandie and won the English crown. A second venture was about to sail from Flanders, where the Rose of York was gathering ships and men. His object was the Irish coast, where he could count on friends in every town. His father, Edward the Fourth, had made him Lord Lieutenant of Ireland. Gloucester, a usurper, could not cancel that appointment; Richmond, also a usurper, could not cancel that appointment. Walters was the mayor of Cork, and Walters was prepared to die for him. But while his ships were loading stores and guns, intelligence from Dover led him to believe that he might march on London from a nearer base. He heard that Kent was full of Yorkist peers; these peers were all his partizans; and he had but to show himself on shore. A dash was therefore to be made at Deal. His venture drained the riff-raff of a dozen ports, and Max, who had not ceased to hate the Tudor prince, was certain that the Duke would win his kingdom. Max was Emperor now; as Emperor, he recognised the "King;" as Emperor he made a treaty with him. Max agreed to help the "King" with men, and Richard promised to assist the Em-

peror in disturbing France. When York was King of England, there should be merry times in Normandie and Maine. The days of Crecy would return, and Max, then resting in a dubious state at Worms, might sleep securely on the Rhine. But in his idle hurry, Max forgot to send the promised aid.

4. A fleet of ships was hired and troops were put on board. The Duchess paid her money, and the Kaiser's lancers were expected. Margaret wrote to Borgia, as the man of God, the soul of justice, praying him to do her nephew right; and the more worldly Max desired his agents in the Papal court to hint that Richard was a better friend to Rome than Henry. Borgia waited for events; in truth, all Europe waited for events. The hour of words was past; the world had judged the Rose of York. From Rome to Stirling, from Granada to Vienna, there was not one reigning prince who deemed the Duke of York a cheat. But Henry had some talent for the field. Was Richard his superior in the art of war? Had he the science which commands success? With fifteen hundred men at arms, and five hundred seamen of all grades on board, the Pretender ran out to sea, and put these questions to the proof. No one had yet forgotten how a little fleet ran out of Harfleur, just ten years ago, and what had come of her adventure. Margaret had relays of couriers at her palace gates, and Philip had despatches sent to him by day and night. In Stirling every one was shouting for a border raid, and James, in hope of picking up some beeves and

horses, if no richer spoil, led out his warriors to the Tweed. At Worms the Kaiser was elate with joy. "We entertain great hope," he said to Contarini, "that the Duke of York, when he has gained his kingdom, will attack the French. We have his promise to that end." In England there was neither fear nor joy; but close, sedate, and pregnant measures of defence. A few hot tongues were wagging here and there in favour of the House of York; but years of peace and settled law, the Queen's devotion to her consort, and the birth of princes who combined the rival claims, induced the sober part of England to accept existing facts. Whatever flaw was in the reigning King, would disappear when Arthur came to wear his crown. A Rose of York meant civil war, and even a successful war meant years of desolating strife. A party of the House of York would raise a party of the House of Lancaster. New Wakefields and St. Albans might be fought, and at the end of forty years a second Bosworth might uncrown the reigning King. Meantime all growth would be disturbed, all law would be suspended. Force and wantonness would riot through the land. A man who honestly believed that Richard was the Duke of York might well deny his right to ravage England for his personal gain. No grinding tyranny drove men to despair. The King was fond of money, and his minister Empson was unpopular in the shires; but on the whole his people were content to eat and sleep, and cultivate their fields in peace. With all his faults of origin, he had one advantage over every Yorkist prince. His child was

Welsh, and in his rise the Welsh were reconciled to English rule. It was a first step towards a union of the various tribes on British ground. In Arthur, York and Lancaster were wedded, and his reign would be a second step towards unity. A people weary of domestic broils was ready to support the King, without inquiring far into the legal right. Even those who wavered were inclined to cast their lot with Henry when they heard that Richard was supported by the King of Scots. Aware of what was passing, Henry gave his orders and departed for the north. He knew the Kaiser and the King of Scots, and set his main array against the Stuart prince.

5. Misled by false reports, the Rose of York proposed to land near Deal, to seize that town, and march on Walmer Castle, as a camp in which to rally the adherents of his house. All Kent was waiting, he believed, to welcome him; and he had only to unfurl his flag in order to possess the shire. Off Deal, he moored his fleet, and sent some companies of Dutch and Spanish troops on shore, with orders to advance on Walmer, occupy the town, and throw out pickets on the London road. When all was safe, he was himself to land. No one opposed the strangers as they took the beach, though many lads in smocks, who carried bills and hooks, were seen about the fields. "Who were they?" asked these lads in smock. "Friends of the House of York!" "What knights and peers were with them?" When the strangers pushed these lads aside, they shoved and swore at them in turn.

More lads in smocks with English bills and hooks ran down the cliffs. A general fight came on. No other strangers landed, but the Rose of York, who stood in readiness to come on shore, could see his troops in mail contending on the beach with lads in smocks. The lads seemed led by men who understood their work. An hour or more the strangers held their ground; but every house in Deal seemed full of bills and hooks; and after fighting stiffly for a time, the foreign troops were broken, captured, and destroyed. Some squads were either piked to death or pushed into the sea; but when the wrecks were gathered into line, a hundred and sixty prisoners answered to the call and gave their names. These names were chiefly Spanish, and the lesson of their capture was a bitter one for Spain. But England was in no light mood of mind. Her peace had been disturbed; her soil had been profaned. She meant to tell free lancers of all nations what they had to face by landing in an English shire. The prisoners, roped in gangs, were marched from Deal to London, with a hangman at their side, who bared their backs, and whipped them as they limped and groaned along the dusty roads. In London, they were tried as pirates, and condemned to hang in chains. One batch was strung on Dover cliff; a second batch was strung on Harwich sands; and every fort and nose of land in front of Flanders was adorned with German and Castillian bones.

6. Much cowed in spirit, the Pretender set his compass for the Irish coast, where he expected to be welcomed with a burst of frantic joy. The Irish

were his earliest friends, and Ireland was devoted to the House of York. The citizens of Cork were faithful, and his warmest partizan, John Walters, was in office. Yet, the King was well prepared for him in County Cork. Prince Henry, five years old, had been appointed Lord Lieutenant, with Sir Edward Poynings as his deputy, and Father Henry Deane as chancellor. Edward Poynings was a soldier, and the deputy of Calais. Henry Deane was an Augustine monk, a man of venerable aspect, and the Prior of Llanthonia in Wales. Each in his several office was a man of high capacity and perfect trust. An English army had been sent with Poynings, and an English bench had followed Deane. The whole administration had been placed in English hands. A new treasurer, a new chief justice, a new chief baron, were appointed. These judicious officers had curbed the Yorkist peers and crushed the restless kernes. No fuss was shown; but every man was in his place. Sir Robert Cotton stood to sea with a considerable fleet. Henry Wyat had the musters out for drill. Kildare had been removed, and that so craftily, that no one, even among his Irish tenants, pitied him. He was a prisoner of the Church!

7. An Irish parliament having voted him a traitor to his sovereign, Poynings might have seized him as a prisoner of the State; but Father Henry, whose capacity for secular business was astonishing, contrived that he should seem to be a prisoner of the Church. John Payne, the bishop of Meath, had been the Irish chieftain's early friend. They

had been out with Simnel; Payne having preached the coronation sermon at Christ Church, while Kildare was raising armies to support the Rose of York. When Payne received a pardon, he had gone to London, where he sought and gained a pardon for his still more guilty mate. Some Irish feud had parted these old plotters, whose dislike had now become as fervid as their love had formerly been warm. Kildare had tried to kill the bishop. One day he had set a church on fire, and many persons fancied he had done so in the hope that Payne was in the church. Another day he followed Payne into his chancel, loud in oath and sword in hand. Payne dropt upon his knee before an altar, and the furious Earl exclaimed, "By St. Bridget, were it not for fear my prince would be offended with me, I would lay this sword across your shaven pate." Kildare laid hands on Payne, and carrying him to his castle, kept him prisoner, till the deputy, Poynings, called for his release. Kildare consented to release the bishop, but insisted on the promise of a pardon. Treating faithless men with faithless measures, Poynings sent Kildare a promise, got him into Dublin, seized him in the dead of night, and putting him on board a bark, despatched him into England as a man accused of sacrilege. Payne had to follow him as witness, and the Yorkist peer and Yorkist prelate were detained in London till the King could find a day to hear their case. The bishop was received at court; Kildare was lodged for safety in the Tower. A personal feud, the right or wrong of which no tongue could tell, had left the partizans of York without their secular and spiritual chiefs.

8. No blaze of fire along the Irish hills gave signals for the foreign troops to land. At every port an English cross was floating in the wind. In every cove and inlet watch was kept. In every shire the musters were at drill. Kildare and Payne being gone, no Yorkist peer but Desmond was prepared to take a leading part. Kildare was hostage for the Butlers and O'Briens, no less than for the Geraldines. Payne, too, was in the tyrant's power. The factions seemed to lie beneath a spell. A country filled with Yorkist peers and knights could hardly trail a pike, or even raise a shout for "Richard!" when he came to them acknowledged by his aunt, supported by the Kaiser and the King of Scots, and favoured in their secret councils by the Kings of France and Spain. Unable to advance by way of Cork, an inland city, the Pretender listened to advice. John Walters had not cooled in zeal, and Desmond was prepared to risk his life. But where were they to strike a blow? Suppose they made a dash at Waterford? It was a royal burgh; a gateway opening up the country; and the nearest port to Milford Haven. Waterford in their hands would be a tower of strength. Here Henry the Second had descended when he came to take possession of the isle. But nine miles from the sea, Waterford was easily approached by sea. Their friends from Cork could help in the assault by land. All parties joined in this advice. Desmond and Walters were to storm the gates, while the Pretender forced a passage up the Suir.

CHAPTER VI.

An Impostor!

1495.

1. THIS failure fortified the throne on every side. Let Duchess Margaret either rail or weep, her grandson Philip had to make some show of friendship for his able and offended neighbour. Never doubting that the Rose of York was Margaret's nephew, Philip was prepared to help his cousin at the proper season; but he owed some duty to his Flemish states, as well as to the House of York. A Duke in Bruges and Ghent, he had to study how he was to live in peace with one who had the power to injure Bruges and Ghent. Restrictions had been placed by Henry on the trade with Flanders, and restrictions on the Flemish trade was ruin to the shippers, bankers, and craftsmen of his towns. Nor was he safe from more direct attacks. An English fleet stood on and off his coasts; an English army lay at Calais, Guisnes, and Hamme. A Kaiser might indulge in sneers at Henry, for a King of England could not send his fleet to Worms and Spires; but Henry's ships were visible from Flushing; and a neighbour who had troops at Guisnes and fleets off Flushing might become a dangerous ally to his factious citizens in Bruges. The King of Scots, now pressed beyond

the Tweed, beheld himself alone, with all the troops of England in his front. He sought relief in Margaret Drummond's smiles; but bonny Margaret Drummond could not witch away the English horse and foot. James tried to soothe the English court, and Henry, ever prudent, was inclining towards a policy of peace and union with the Scots. The seeds of an idea which were soon to bear much fruit were sprouting in his mind. Even Max himself, though he would bate no jot of his belief that Richard was King Edward's son, consented to receive Sir John Egremont as the usurper's envoy, and to treat with him about a league—a league which was of much concern to Max and Germany—against the King of France.

2. In spite of all his sister's warnings, Charles had led his armies through the Alps, and, strange to say, an enterprise which every one had called a crazy act, had opened with a blaze of glory and success. The state of Italy, where almost every city was at feud with her immediate neighbour, and the chief republics were at variance with the Holy See, had favoured Charles. Dynastic struggles dyed the streets of Florence, Milan, and Perugia, with civic blood. Rome was quarrelling with Naples. Genoa was at strife within herself. Pisa had been overthrown by war; Siena had been overthrown by peace. The princes were intriguing to destroy each other, and the Church was struggling to annex their states. Pietro de Medici had signed a secret treaty with the King of Naples. Lodovico il Moro had contracted an alliance with the Doge of Venice and the

Pope of Rome. Savonarola, the Dominican, had begun to call for his Reform, and point the moral of his sermons by referring to the scandalous conduct of his spiritual chief. Loud voices called upon the French to intervene, some patriots even begged the Turks to save the country from herself. The King of France had answered to their call. Descending from the Alps, as friends of every cause, the French had entered Florence, Rome, and Naples. Italy had fallen at their feet, and Charles, who panted for another world to conquer, had begun to throw his glances into Greece. French agents were already in the isles, and Charles, puffed out with sudden vanity, assumed to be as much the lord of Athens as he was of Rome. The Doge of Venice took alarm; the King of Spain had still more cause to be alarmed. As Duke of Athens, King of Sicily, and heir of Naples, he had everything at stake. If Charles should carry out his schemes of conquest, Sicily would not be safe. Fernando broached the project for a league of all the kingdoms and republics menaced by the French; a Holy League he called it, since he meant to brand the French as enemies of the Catholic Church. These kingdoms and republics were prepared. Illusions were no longer possible. Instead of helping every one, as the Italians dreamt, the French had only helped themselves. As city after city opened to receive the strangers, she had bitterly repented of her sin against the commonweal. Plate, pictures, money, everything the strangers wanted from a wealthy and artistic country, they had taken with unsparing hand. Italian causes had been left alone; and nothing had been done by Charles excepting for the pride and gain of France. But soon the day for flight and perfidy had come. The Pope deserted Charles; then Lodovico turned against him. Barbarigo, Doge of Venice, joined the league of princes. Kaiser Max came in; for Max was threatened with a rival in imperial rank. Charles wanted to be Emperor, and since he could not take the style of Charles the Great, he fancied he might take the style of Constantine the Fourth. A throne, he said, was vacant. Max was Emperor of the West; Charles would be Emperor of the East. But Max denied that any throne was vacant; he being Emperor both of West and East. In wrath and haste a Holy League was formed. Five signatures were appended; those of Rome, Germany, Spain, Venice, and Milan. Max would only sign the articles on condition that his colleagues styled him Emperor of the East as well as of the West. The Holy League being made, Gonsalvo passed into Calabria, and began to press the victors. Charles, abandoned by the princes he had favoured and the cities he had plundered, rode into the north. He passed through Rome in silence; and in Lombardy he ran against Italian pikes. French gallantry preserved him in the field; but every day his hold on Italy was loosened; and the fruits of all his efforts were at stake. His troops were fighting bravely, but the French had no man in the south to measure weapons with Gonsalvo. Charles was wavering in his plans; and Max was thinking that if Henry could be drawn into the Holy League, the French would have to call their troops across the Alps. He would have gladly done without this aid; but France was so alert and quick that he was never at his ease. He, therefore, deigned to hear Sir John, although, more knight than emperor, he could hardly tame his tongue in presence of the English knight.

3. The Rose of York being gone, Kildare was brought before the council, and his enemy Payne, the Irish bishop, was placed before him at the board. "What say you?" asked the King. "My liege," Kildare replied, "the Bishop is a learned man, which I am not, and therefore he will easily outdo me in the argument." "Then choose a counsel," said the King. "I doubt," rejoined Kildare, "if I shall have the good fellow whom I choose." "By my troth, you shall," the King assured him. "Give me your hand," the Irish peer entreated. "Here is my hand," said Henry, laughing; "when will you choose your counsellor?" "Never," interposed the Irish prelate: "never, if he has his choice." "Thou liest, brallagh, bald bishop! I will choose a counsellor as soon as thou wouldst choose a fair wench, if thou couldst have thy wish—within an hour." The council roared; and Henry, turning to Kildare, inquired, "Can such a thing be true?" "By your hand," replied Kildare, taking Henry by the palm, "there is not in London such a mutton-master as yon shaven priest. I know him well." "It is best you choose your counsellor well," said Henry; "I perceive he will have much to do." "Shall I choose him now?" the Irish peer inquired. "Yes; if you think good," replied the King. Kildare assured him

he would have the best in England. "Aye, and who is that?" cried Henry. "Marry," said Kildare, "the King himself! and by St. Bridget I will choose no other." Henry broke into his winsome laugh. "A wiser man," he whispered, "might have chosen worse." Some witnesses deposed that he had set a church on fire. "I did it—that is true," he sighed; "but by my troth I would never have done it, but I thought the bishop was in the church." The grey-beards at the council had to hold their sides. "All Ireland," murmured Payne, "cannot rule this man." "Then let him rule all Ireland," laughed the King. And Henry meant in earnest what he said in fun. Kildare was courting Bessie St. John, Henry's cousin of the Beauchamp blood; and having won that lady's heart, he married her, became a member of the royal circle, and was chosen as the Prince's Deputy. Having made an English servant of the Irish peer, the King had no more trouble with the Geraldines.

4. But more than all, a change was evident on the side of Spain. When Richard was preparing ships and men, the King and Queen of Spain had felt so doubtful of the future that they sent for Puebla, and proposed to cancel the agreement, and declare the treaty as to Catharine at an end. To them the Tudor king was nothing; to their daughter, Arthur of Winchester was nothing. England was the prize they sought. If prudence bade them wait before they took so strong a step, they held a haughty and exacting language at the English Court. A minister of rank whom they had promised, in the

room of Puebla, was not sent. The cripple crossed the sea, instructed to assume a haughty tone, and ask for things that Henry could not grant. The King was to be told that Spain had signed a separate treaty with the French. He was to be reminded of his duty to the Pope. He was to be informed that Max was angry with him, and that Spain alone could turn aside from him the Kaiser's wrath. The Kaiser he must learn, was King of Kings, and no man was a King unless the Kaiser recognized his rank. These proud beginnings had a more offensive close. Should Henry speak of Catharine, Puebla was to listen and report; but he was not to say one word implying that the articles of marriage were in force. Those articles were not regarded by the King and Queen of Spain as still in force. "All former treaties are annulled," Fernando wrote in his instructions to his minister; but feeling that his pen was giving an unwonted outline to his thought, he blotted out the words, and left that minister to guess his secret mind.

5. So long as the Pretender stood at sea Fernando had been silent and reserved. No sign from him enlightened Puebla, who had nothing but the blotted line, "all former treaties are annulled," to guide him in his intercourse with Fox and Morton. Innocence, as Puebla knew, would plead in vain with either king or queen of Spain; but the Pretender was a single man, and if he won the crown he would require a bride. Though Isabel kept her counsels, Henry learnt that she was corresponding with his rival, and he spoke to Puebla of her breach

of faith. The Kaiser he could understand; the Kaiser was a son-in-law of Duchess Margaret; his children were conspicuous members of the House of York; but Isabel of Spain was a Lancastrian princess, and was fighting with him in their common cause. His son was hers, her daughter his; and to encourage Perkin was to rob their children of a crown. The Queen had answered curtly, that she had not written to Him of York. "El de Ayorque" was a title hit upon by her. The Kaiser called his cousin Prince of York; the French and Flemings called him Duke of York; and Isabel edged between these several styles. She recognised him as a member of the House of York while she withheld from him the rank of Prince and Duke.

6. But on the news of his defeat, the Queen turned round at once. Let Richard be as graceful and as witty as a fairy prince, she saw that he was wanting in the first condition of success in arms. He could not fight. His rival on the English throne, although a man of peace, had shown some talent, and his courage was beyond dispute. The King being likely to maintain his ground, she must be prudent in her speech, and less exacting in her tone. The cripple was instructed to approach the King with an assurance that his masters had not written to the so-called Duke of York. If they had written to the Duchess Margaret, as the King complained, they had but done so to inform her highness that the man she sheltered was a rogue.

7. All parties now began to court the prince whose crown so many of them would have given to

"him of York." The Pope appointed Puebla his ambassador in London. Max sent over a commissioner to treat about the Holy League, and Charles, intent on winning sympathy for France, supplied his Portuguese story of the Rose of York. Fernando could not lag behind. On hearing of the stuff sent over by the French, he wrote to London that if Henry wanted proofs about the barber, he could furnish more and stronger evidence than the King of France. He had the means for getting at all facts in Lisbon. "We can send the King," Fernando wrote to Puebla, "written evidence of many persons who knew the boy; among others, that of Ruy de Sousa, who lived in London during part of King Edward's reign, and often at that period saw the Duke of York." Unhappily, these stories of the Lisbon barber smote the tale already published by the English council. If the youth were Portuguese, he could not be a Fleming also. If his father was a Lisbon barber, he was not a water-bailiff at Tournai. Of two such stories one, at least, was false, and Henry saw no reason to refute his former tale.

8. A witness was secured in Pregent Menou, who had brought the prince from Portugal to Cork. If any other man than Tyrrell knew the truth about him, Menou was that other man. Menou had been with him in Lisbon; Menou had presented him to Walters, Mayor of Cork; Menou had seen the whole intrigue with Desmond and Kildare. If York were an impostor, Menou could supply the proofs. If York were a Plantagenet, Menou could do more

than any one alive, excepting Tyrrell, to supply the proofs. In either case the Breton trader was a man to gain. The King made haste to win his confidence. He granted him three hundred pounds in gold; he settled him on Irish lands; he gave him letters of denization; he enriched him by a patent for exporting wool. He took the man into his service, and invested him with an important trust. A few months after the Pretender failed in Waterford, Henry appointed Menou Constable of Carrickfergus Castle. But he never called on him to tell the public what he knew about the Rose of York.

CHAPTER VII.

The Child of Sin.

1495-6.

1. WHILE Isabel was waiting for events to guide her as to Catharine, she was suddenly bereaved of her first councillor, the Cardinal of Spain. She liked Mendoza, and in sickness made herself his nurse. Being near him as he lay in pain, she learned that in his trials he was haunted by the spectre which had troubled her so long. That fair young queen, whose mother they had killed, whose honour they had stained, whose birthright they had filched, whose person they had seized and thrust into a foreign cell, was near the Cardinal in his latest hours on earth. No blaze of tapers drove that phantom from his bed; nor could he die in peace till he had spoken with the Queen, his partner in those unforgotten crimes. He had repented of his evil deeds. Mendoza was too good a man to dwell without remorse on all that he had done. A scholar and a prelate, he had never given his sympathy to inquisitors. If proud and worldly, he had not been wanton in his exercise of power, and he had made no war on learning and on learned men. But Isabel had lured him from the path of duty to his lawful queen, and he had sold his conscience for the empty name of Cardinal-

King. At length the inner voices rose and would be heard. What price shall pay a man to lose his soul? The dying Cardinal begged the Queen to think of what was past; and, for the sake of his salvation and her own, to study how she might undo the mischief they had wrought.

2. Five years ago, the Cardinal had carried Doña Isabel, the Child of Sin, to Portugal, and paid her down to John the Perfect, as the wages of his shame. Her nuptials had been splendid, but Affonzo, who was younger than herself, had faded from the presence of his gloomy bride. The Prince had passed away in early youth, and left no heir behind. John's dream of a united Spain was gone; his house was childless; and his sceptre would descend upon a younger branch. He never rallied from the blow. Some stings of conscience pricked him when he thought of that fair woman—bone of his own bone and flesh of his own flesh—whom he had wronged to gratify the mistress of Castille. He could not help but think of her, for in his desolate house, as well as in his angry capital, every voice was crying that Affonzo's early death was nothing but a judgment of offended Heaven. A curse had fallen on the kingdom, and a low and sullen pride embittered all the intercourse of Portugal with Spain. John sang no hymn of gladness when Granada fell. He gave some pity to the noble Moor, and granted an asylum to the persecuted Jew. When Isabel insisted that the holy race should be expelled from every part of Spain, the King of Portugal, alike in protest and in policy, received the fugitives in his towns and ports:

—a great and noble act, which cancelled many of the errors of a feeble life. Zacuto, the astronomer, became a friend of Manoel, Duke of Beja, heir presumptive to the throne. Aboab, the learned Rabbi, found a second Israel in the states of John the Perfect. Many a bitter tear was dried, and many a bleeding wound was closed, by these concessions of the Portuguese; but every deed of mercy on the part of John estranged him more than ever from the Queen of Spain.

3. A widow in her bridal year, the Child of Sin had come to Spain a worn and blighted creature—blighted in her birth and in her marriage, and afraid lest what so many tongues were saying of her husband's death was true. She moped and moaned about the court; alarmed at her own shade; averse to either see or to be seen; a living spectre in the royal house. Mendoza saw his work undone. Instead of Portugal being linked with Spain, the sovereigns and the people were at feud. A dying man, Mendoza saw his life unrolled before his eyes. The evil of his course was now too plain. So far as evil deeds can be removed, he sought to have his evil deeds removed. A dying priest, Mendoza urged his old and favourite policy on the Queen. The Excellenta might be married to her son. Don Juan's consort might return to Spain, and re-ascend her father's throne. Mendoza begged the Queen to weigh his words—his final words to her on earth. "The good man wanders in his mind, and chatters like an idiot," she exclaimed, as her now penitent partner passed into another world.

CHAP. VII.—THE CHILD OF SIN. 1495-6.

4. John the Perfect followed in Mendoza's wake. No sooner was his son Affonzo dead than he began to pine away, and on his dying bed he, too, became a victim of remorse. Mendoza's sin was on his soul. Unable to endure the pangs of conscience, he inquired for Manoel, Duke of Beja, his successor. John and Manoel had been much estranged. Distracted by Affonzo's death, the King had striven to set the Duke aside; but he had failed to dispossess the lawful prince; and when his end was near, he sent for Manoel to his room. Much talk the cousins held about the Excellenta. John repented him of many things; and begged the Duke, as his successor on the throne, to help in setting right the things which pressed so heavily on his heart. But most of all he spoke about the royal Nun. "Let earthly passions tempt you as they may, you seek to do Juana right," he said; and in the hope of finding peace, the royal sinner turned him to the wall and died.

5. A liberal prince, who bore in after years the name of Fortunate, Manoel was in the pride of youth and strength, and men of twenty-six are apt to pay scant heed to dying prayers. While he was Duke of Beja only, he had sought the hand of Lady Anne, a younger sister of the English Queen; but Anne had little more to bring him than her high descent and the incomparable beauty of her race; and when Affonzo died he saw within his reach a greater prize. Affonzo's moping widow was a princess of Castille. Her brother was a feeble lad, and if that feeble lad should die, the moping widow would be

Queen of Spain. To win her was to win a crown, and what was more in Manoel's eyes, the prospect of uniting Spain and Portugal in one vast kingdom, reaching from the Straits of Hercules to the mountains of Navarre. But he could only win that moping widow at a price; the price of doing, like John, a jailer's office towards his cousin in her convent cell. His choice was quickly made. He chose the path of profit and disgrace; forgot the dying king's injunctions; set a double watch on Santa Clara; and in asking for the Child of Sin, assured her mother he had seen and loved the princess when she was his nephew's wife!

6. The moping widow was alarmed. At twenty-five she was an aged female; having lost the taste of youth, and only wishing to devote her days to prayer, beneath some convent roof. Even if her heart could fill with love, her uncle Manoel would not be the man whom she could bear to wed. A niece and uncle were forbidden by the law to marry. Though the Pope might grant a dispensation from the penalties of sin, still sin would be committed, and a woman of her birth and temper shrank from such a course. Already she had too much sin to bear. Nor was the Queen, her mother, less alarmed. Too well she knew what Manoel sought; too well she knew that he would press his suit; too well she knew that if he urged her she would have to yield. A man who held the Excellenta under lock and key had Isabel and all her kingdoms in his grasp. On seeing that the moping widow would not marry, and that Manoel must be gained some

other way, the Queen proposed to send her younger daughter, Doña Maria, to the court of Lisbon. Maria was a younger and a prettier woman than her sister; but the King of Portugal would not take the younger and the prettier bride. Maria was the youngest child but one. Three lives already stood between her and the crown; the lives of Juan, Isabel, and Juana. Juan was a pallid youth, now entering on his eighteenth year, and pallid youths of eighteen are not sure to fail. Isabel was hardly twenty-six, and moping widows have been known to make a second choice. Juana, now fifteen, was strong in frame as she was brisk in mind. Whoever failed, Juana seemed a likely girl to live. Maria's chance of coming to the crown was slight, and Manoel hoped to grasp his prize at once. If Doña Isabel had been either dead or under vows, he might have been content to take the second daughter, Fair Juana, as the next in order to Don Juan, even though this second daughter of the Queen was not a favourite of Dominicans like the Child of Sin.

CHAPTER VIII.

Fair Juana.

1496.

1. JUANA, the most lovely, agile, and enlightened of the royal sisters, was in high disfavour with the brethren of St. Dominic. Juana was of other mood than Isabel. Although she knelt at mass and read her book of saints, she had no fancy for the company of coarse and ignorant friars, and when she listened to the homilies of Fray Andreas, her confessor, it was often with a pouting and impatient face. A beaming eye and baby ways were in her favour; but the Queen, her mother, listening to the monks, grew angry with her wayward child; in whom she saw to her dismay a something of the genius of her liberal brother and the beauty of her uncrowned niece. Nor were her fears without a cause. Suppose her feeble son and moping daughter were to fail? Juana was the next in order of succession, and in course of nature would be Queen of Spain. But she and the inquisitors could not live in peace. Juana might essay to put them down. How far the friars would go, if they had reason to believe the Church in danger, she was well aware. The monks were stronger now than in Enrique's days. Besides, there was the royal Nun — a nun who had not

taken vows, and who might raise her flag at any time. How would her child be able to resist the popular feeling for her niece? This source of danger must be stopped; and, whether she should bend or break in the experiment, her daughter must be reconciled to that great party which had made her Queen.

2. A sterner spirit than Mendoza sat beside her chair, in Fray Francisco Ximenes, Primate of Castille and Cardinal of Spain. Excepting natural gifts, this friar had scarcely anything in common with Mendoza. He was not of noble birth; he had no taste for luxury; he ate no dainty food; he wore no purple; he disdained to ride on mules. In early life he often wanted bread. His father placed him at the school of Alcala, from which he went to Salamanca, and from thence to Rome, where he had won the eye of Sixtus the Fourth. A prodigy of learning, he had studied with success, not only letters and theology, not only civil law and criminal law, but various Oriental tongues. Yet many years elapsed before the low-born sage could win his way to rank and power. At last, he won them by appearing to reject them. Laying down his poor preferment in the priesthood, he became a brother of the Order of St. Francis in Toledo, where he roused the city by his sermons, and secured her notice by retiring to a convent in a wood. A crowd went out to see him and confess to him. Mendoza, hearing of a man who lived a holy life and drew the city after him, presented him at court. Ximenes saw his kingdom made. At fifty-six he

was confessor to the Queen, at fifty-nine Archbishop of Toledo, and the Cardinal of Spain. At once he stamped his image on the court and on the church. Austere and self-denying, he declared that offices should not be given to those who sought them. "A request for place," he said, "implies either want of modesty or want of merit." Like the great Dominican in Florence, he commenced reforms on every side; in the religious orders, in the regular clergy, in the convents, in the colleges and schools. He preached the merit of belonging to religious orders. Men who wished to rise became lay brothers of St. Francis; women who desired to shine became lay-sisters of St. Francis. Isabel was a sister. Catalina was a sister. In Mendoza's time a friar bore pike and sword. Ximenes made the fighting-men wear hood and gown. Yet the reform for which his Church has praised Ximenes most, was the example of a holy life. He never bent his eye on woman, and he never grasped at personal wealth. On every side he kept his vow, and lived as he had sworn to live, obedient, chaste, and poor.

3. This priest, whose errors were the outcome of his virtues, was resolved on winning over the Mohammedan people of Granada to the faith of Christ. Fernando had agreed in his capitulations with the citizens to respect their customs, laws, and creeds; and he was not unwilling to maintain his royal pledges. It was hardly safe to rouse the passions of the conquered race. Some risings had already taken place, in consequence of a flagrant breach of the conditions made between the Moors

and the Castillian Knights. But then Ximenes had not signed that treaty with the Moors, nor was he bound by what the knights had signed. At first, he tried a gentle treatment. Sending for the learned Moors, he made them fervid speeches, and presented them with costly gifts. Some few he won by speech and gift; but with the hard of heart he tried the virtue of arrest, confinement, and starvation. As the work went slowly forward, he imagined he might gain his ends by burning all the Moorish books. Then came a deed which rivalled and revenged the act of Omar in the capital of Egypt. From afar and near he gathered in the treasures of Arabian learning—books of science, books of poetry, books of travel, books of history—original, adapted and translated — and in tens of thousand burnt them all!

4. Austere and jealous, he committed Doña Juana to a body of observant friars, with Fray Andreas at their head. Andreas undertook the task of bringing her into a better frame. A stiff and swarthy man, who boasted that he was not worth a pin, and yet was happier with his mouldy crust than kings who dined on costly meat and wines, he locked the princess in her chamber, read to her the lives of saints, and took away some portion of her daily food. He put her under penance, and at last he broke her to his will. But she was cowed, not crushed. A sullen fire was burning in her heart; she yielded only in her words; and Isabel, her mother, no less troubled by the peril of her state on earth than by the danger to her soul in heaven,

grew sore in heart against her beautiful and petulant child.

5. This stage of suffering ended with Juana's marriage to the Austrian Archduke, Philip the Fair; a fact that was to change the course and aspect of events, to plant a German dynasty on the throne of Spain, and lay the platform for a universal empire under Charles the Fifth.

CHAPTER IX.

Spanish Marriages.

1496.

1. WHEN Charles of France, rejecting Marguerite and marrying Duchess Anne, had challenged Germany to mortal strife, Fernando, seizing on the moment of imperial frenzy, had proposed a league of Spain and Germany against the French. It was to be a large and lasting league; a bond between their houses and their kingdoms; so that what was done by King and Kaiser should be carried forward by their sons and by their sons' sons through all coming time. Juan, Prince of the Asturias, was to marry Marguerite, the bright and witty creature driven away by Charles; while Philip, Archduke of Austria, was to wed Juana, fairest daughter of the house of Spain. Fernando meant to marry Germany as he had married Portugal. If Max were made a partner in his crime against his cousin, the Señora Excellenta, nothing need be feared from her. If Marguerite were Queen of Spain, as Juan's bride, the Emperor would become as much a partner in that crime as John of Portugal had been. The Emperor had listened to these Spanish offers with a greedy sense. To marry provinces and kingdoms was the habit of his house:—

> Bella gerant alii, tu felix Austria nube
> Nam quæ Mars aliis, dat tibi regna Venus!

2. Fernando made things pleasant at the Austrian court. Max had no money to bestow on Marguerite; yet feared to let the Spaniards get a footing in the Netherlands and on the Alps. Artois and Franche Comté ought never to be parted from the empire. If the French had carried out their treaty, these important provinces would have gone to France; but having got them back from Charles, the Emperor feared to let them fall into another hand. Yet Marguerite could hardly go without a portion let her marry whom she might. Fernando showed the Kaiser how to marry his child without giving her a ducat or an acre. Let there be a pure exchange of brides. Let each forego the woman's share. More knight than emperor, Max snapt at the proposal, for the chief advantage of the bargain lay with him. His daughter was to enter Spain without a portion; and Juana was to enter Germany without a portion; so far King and Kaiser stood in line. But Marguerite was to yield her artificial interest in the coronets of Artois and Franche Comté, while Juana could not yield her natural interest in the crowns of Aragon and Castille.

3. Doña Juana sailed for Flanders, and the fleet which bore her from Laredo carried the Archduchess Marguerite to Spain. Philip the Fair, a youth with yellow hair and light blue eyes, whose beauty was a little marred by his long Austrian lip, received his bride with rapture, and was true to her a summer day. The bridal feast was spread at Lille, and

artists of all nations were employed to celebrate the nuptial rites. Juana found at Ghent a liberal church, with priests who laughed at friars, who read the newly-printed books, and preached the free theology in vogue among the French. As yet she saw no writing on the wall; but sharp and menacing eyes were turned on her from Santa Cruz. Don Juan and Marguerite were married in the town of Burgos, with a more than royal state. The pale and sombre boy was smitten by the wit and beauty of his bride, a girl who laughed and sang the live-long day; but his confessor and his almoner, brethren of St. Dominic and St. Francis, were alarmed by Marguerite's happy ways, so different from the stiff and dismal habits of the Spanish court. The boy, who had never breathed the air of freedom and enjoyment till he met his airy consort, fell into a trance of dizzy and delighted love.

4. While all these bridal feasts were on, the King of Portugal pressed his suit in terms which could no longer be put off with words. He would not have the younger girl. He wanted Isabel, and would not be denied. The moping widow, listening to the counsels of her mother, put him to a test. He said he loved her; would he make a sacrifice for her? A lover would do anything to gain the woman of his choice. What would he do for her? Would he forget for her the liberal passion of his youth and yield his conscience to the brethren of St. Dominic? If so, she would accept his hand. But he must give a striking proof of his submission

to the order. He must set aside the noblest act of John, and drive the Jews from Portugal as thoroughly as they had been expelled from Spain. A fearful test; but not a test of love! He felt no love, and had to make no sacrifice for love. His yearnings were for crowns. He cared no more for Doña Isabel than he had cared for Lady Anne. Could he destroy for his ambition twenty thousand happy homes? Could he drive out a hundred thousand men and women from his kingdom? Could he force into his caravels, to sail they knew not why and whither, multitudes of aged men, of innocent girls, and unoffending babes?

5. To Manoel's shame he yielded to the woman's bait. A royal edict bade the Jews depart from Portugal. No one, however great in science and in favour, was to lag behind. Zacuto had to quit his globes; Aboab had to carry off his scrolls. Scant time was given them to prepare for exile. Such as had not gone in time were to be seized, baptized, and marked as converts. The Dominicans hoped to catch a crowd of laggers, and in order to delay their going they were forced to leave the country from a single port. The roads were rough, the caravels were few. Young children sickened on the road and died. A few of the unhappy race were left behind; the sick, the aged, and the halt; yet even these were few; for in this awful scene, which Usque calls a final Exodus, the rich and vigorous helped the poor and weak. At length they got on board their ships. At sea, they parted company; some going north towards Flanders, others dropping

south towards Africa, and many running up the midland sea to Venice and the Grecian Isles. To Portugal they left a bitter and abiding curse.

6. The Jews being ousted from his kingdom, Manoel claimed his price, the first-born child of Spain. Although her marriage with his nephew had been called a "curse," he would not wait for her one day beyond his time. To get her, he had parted from his friend Zacuto. Caring more for science than for anything on earth save rule and government, he had robbed his country of the lights of learning and the masters of finance and industry in order to obtain her hand. A gambler who had staked his fortune on a throw, could not have been more anxious to possess his gains. The moping widow was obliged to yield. With heavy heart she bade her sisters, Catalina and Maria, her adieux, and rode with her parents to the frontier city of Valencia, where she gave the King of Portugal her frigid hand and lifeless heart. He made no fuss about his love, but took her for the prize she was; a woman only one remove from twenty crowns. In wedding her, he wedded her contingent claims. With neither royal feast nor public show, with neither private hope nor personal love, the Child of Sin, the curse of Portugal, took her rank and place as Manoel's wife. Her parents were content; Fernando that the royal Nun was safe, and Isabel that the Hebrews were expelled. But while they ate the nuptial feast, the curse began to work around them. Riders came in haste from Salamanca, whither Juan had repaired, with news that he had

fallen sick. A chill, a fever, and a wasting sickness were upon him. The physicians were in mortal fear, and if the King and Queen desired to see their son alive, they must be up and in the saddle ere the morning broke!

BOOK THE SIXTH.

PRINCESS OF WALES.

CHAPTER I.

Catalina.

1497.

1. IN these great matches with the Empire, England, Portugal, and Flanders, Catharine's parents touched the zenith of their fortunes. They could stretch their hands from sea to sea. The Caliphs of Granada were expelled. The liberal party in Castille was crushed. Their Holy Office was at work in every part of Spain. A Genoese adventurer was adding unknown regions to their empire in the west Their troops had entered Naples and supported Rome. They had redeemed their duchies in the Pyrenees. By giving Isabel to Manoel they had sealed their frontier, satisfied the brethren of St. Dominic, and locked the gates of Santa Clara on their niece. By giving Catharine to the Prince of Wales, they had secured an ally who could hold the French in check. By marrying Juan to the Kaiser's daughter they had brought the Empire into close

connexion with their house; by marrying Juana to the Archduke Philip they had given their grandson an imperial throne.

2. Maria, now fifteen, was with her sister Catalina, upwards of eleven, at the Alhambra, living in their golden cage. Maria, though refused by Manoel as a younger child, was kept by Isabel, her mother, in reserve. The policy of Spain required a daughter of the reigning house to be in Portugal, and if the moping widow failed them, who, except Maria, could be sent to Lisbon in her place? Maria was reserved. With Catalina everything seemed fixed. She wore her English name; she was the bride of Arthur of Winchester; she urged against her mother's priests the wishes of her future lord.

3. Ximenes, Cardinal of Spain, admitted Catharine as a sister of the Order of St. Francis, and exacted from her childish lips the customary vows. She bound herself by oath to give back all ill-gotten goods, to live in peace with every one, to spend her days in works of charity, to eat no costly food, to wear no personal gauds, to serve the poor and sick, to teach the ignorant, and to live in palaces the life she might have had to live in convent-cells. These vows were hard to keep, and Catharine never tried to keep them. How, among the ruins of Granada, could a child restore ill-gotten goods? How, in the midst of burning pyres, could she devote her time to acts of mercy? Fasting was a form of piety for which she nursed a strong dislike; the greater since the father of Prince Arthur, wishing her to be stout of frame, had begged her mother to allow her wine

at meals. In sultry Spain, the luxury of earth is water. Wine is fire, and in a caliph's chamber wine is a forbidden drink. But Henry had informed the Queen of Spain that if the Princess was to live in London, she must learn betimes to live on wine.

4. At ten she could not speak a word of either French or English. Henry was enraged at this neglect. Himself a scholar, his sons were being taught whatever it was well for kings and dukes to learn. André, the blind French poet, was appointed to the post of Arthur's tutor. André was a learned man, but learned men were not as yet familiar with Castillian. Save a trader here and there, no Englishman could speak that language. How would Arthur court her? How would Henry and his ministers advise her? How could people come to her on business, courtesy, and service? Would she like to have interpreters between her husband and herself? A separate language meant a separate household; for a princess who could speak no language but Castillian, must provide herself with Spanish servants; a confessor, a dueña, and a keeper of the privy purse. Her servants would be strangers in the land. How would the Prince, her husband, rule these foreign servants in his house? If Catharine could be got to England in her early teens, much trouble might be saved, as she would learn to be an English girl before she would be called an English queen. But in Granada neither King nor Queen was yet aware how far the treaty would be carried out. "All former treaties are annulled," was still Fernando's principle. When circumstances led him to propose a second treaty, with a marriage of the

Prince of Wales and Princess Catharine as the binding article,—a treaty with the Pope, the Emperor, the King and Queen of Spain, the Doge of Venice and the Duke of Milan,—it was agreed between the two Kings that Arthur of Winchester should marry Catharine of Aragon when he came of age, and that the Princess Catharine should be sent to London at the age of twelve. But in the drawing of his articles, Fernando make mistakes of fact which helped him to evade his pledge. He stipulated that his daughter should be sent to England when the Prince of Wales was fourteen years of age, and she was twelve; a date which never could arrive, since she was ten months older than the Prince. This error helped Fernando to detain her three years longer than the stipulated time.

5. When Henry took his place as member of the Holy League, he was already strong enough to make his terms with Germany and Spain. A dozen years of peace had given a vast expansion to his means. His treasury was full; his fleets were strongly manned. In every shire his musters were at drill. A capable and active officer had put his ordnance into working order. The factions had been curbed, if not effaced. The Welsh, so long estranged, were coming into better mood. The Irish septs were quiet, and if knight and kerne still quarrelled in the old domain, they seldom turned their arms against the crown. With Scotland not much progress had been made; for Stirling was a nest of French intrigues, and Arthur's contract with the Spanish princess was opposed by France. But Scotland was a nuisance which

the King could use in reckoning with the league. On joining Kaiser, King and Pope, he asked to be excepted from those articles which obliged the leaguers to support each other by a fixed number of men. They yielded to his terms. He asked to be excepted from the article which bound all leaguers to contribute certain sums. Again they yielded to his terms. He asked to be excepted from the article which compelled the leaguers to maintain an army ready to repel aggressions. And again they yielded to his terms. Fernando's blotted line, "All former treaties are annulled," was turned by him against the Spaniards, and the treaty of alliance was renewed on terms more favourable to the English crown.

6. "If Henry joins the League all other members will defend him in his states against every one who seeks to do him harm," Fernando wrote to Puebla while the King was pausing ere he signed. A rumour reached the King of Spain that French ecclesiastics were in London, striving to seduce the King by offers of a princess for his son with a far richer dowry than Catalina was to have. The tale was true; for Charles, being pressed on every side, was eager to connect his fortunes with so strong a friend. At once Fernando wrote to London: "Let the King beware of these French offers; such a match as that proposed would light a flame in England that would quickly burn up Henry and his whole estate." Events near home were lending a most serious meaning to Fernando's promises and threats, for Richard, Duke of York, was in the field again, supported by the personal efforts and the whole resources of the King

of Scots. Again the factions were astir. Again the borders were disturbed, and many of the border chiefs were plotting with the Rose of York. No man could say how soon the storm would burst, how far the ravage might extend. All Henry's hopes of a pacific union of the nations seemed to melt away, and in the place of sending to the north his doves of peace, he must unkennel and unslip his dogs of war. Fernando and his allies had the power to help him and to thwart him in a policy the nearest to his heart.

CHAPTER II.

King of Scots.

1497.

1. ERE Henry joined the Holy League French agents had been sent to Leith, where James was but too eager in their master's cause. For France had always been his patron; and whenever England was at war, her border lay exposed to sudden raids. Some Scots were burning to recover Berwick; more were bent on lifting kine and sheep. To James, the port of Berwick was what Calais was to Charles; an open portal into his estate. Not fifteen years ago that portal lay in Scottish hands; but while the country had been struggling with Albany, an English force had slipt into the town, and could not be expelled. In strength, in shipping, in revenue, Berwick had been a shield of safety and a mine of riches to the northern crown. To get this fortress back, the Scots were ready to engage in war, and since the titular Duke of York agreed to yield that fort, if James would help him to obtain his crown, a bargain was arranged between the King and Duke. The Rose of York appeared at Stirling, and the Scottish cryers ran into the hills with pipe and torch, announcing that the King was girding on his sword, and calling on the clans to arm. These

clans were but too eager for a raid which promised them free quarters in a comfortable English shire.

2. Like every one who met him, James was fascinated by the Rose of York, and his relations with the young pretender ripened into close and passionate regard. James took the stranger to his heart, as well as to his house. He carried him through his towns as something nearer than a royal guest. He put his cousin, Catharine Gordon, in his way, and when the Duke, enchanted by her grace and loveliness, proposed to her in one of the prettiest love-letters in the world, James gave away this daughter of a line of kings to Richard, Duke of York, with rapture. Lady Catharine was a bright and delicate woman, whom her enemy, the Tudor prince, respected for her sense even more than for her miseries; yet her princely instincts never warned her that the husband of her fancy was a low-born churl. She took him, in the "purple light of youth;" she gave her heart into his keeping; and she clung to him through all the tempests of his life. Events had no effect on Lady Catharine's love. Great princes might betray her lord; but Catharine could not change her mind. She never doubted that her partner was King Edward's younger son.

3. Old spears were dragged from wall and gate; old swords were cleaned and ground; old guns were dragged from tower and yard; and the clansmen gathered from the farthest isles. A ship brought men and arms from Duchess Margaret. An agent came from France, professing a desire to mediate, but secretly intending to assist the King of Scots

and Duke of York. Some border families—Nevills, Dacres, Herons—sent to hail the Duke, and James concluded from these merry openings that his guest had but to show his face across the border for the English towns to rise. How little either of them knew about those border lands!

3. His feet on English ground, the Rose of York put out a proclamation in the name of Richard the Fourth, denouncing Henry Tudor as a Welshman, and his councillors as low-born caitiffs. Richard Fox and William Smith, Reginald Bray and Thomas Empson, were among these low-born caitiffs; Fox and Smith being bishops, Bray and Empson councillors and knights. Henry Wyat, Keeper of the Jewels, William Hatcliffe, Secretary of the Exchequer, and Oliver King, Bishop of Bath and Wells, were all denounced by name. Henry was proclaimed a murderer and usurper, a taxer of the people, and an enemy of the Church. The "King" was lavish of his promises of a happier rule; but in the border shires these promises were read in the wild light of blazing farms. Then English blood grew hot against a man who came to free them with a gang of Flemings, French, and Scots. The people rose. A border war broke out; a war conducted in the border style. Being masters in the open field, the clansmen wreaked their rage on farm and peel, until the Duke, distracted by the riot, turned his face away in shame from men whose only deeds were lifting cattle in his name and tossing stolen liquor in his cause. But when he checked them, they began to waver in their faith. Even James in-

dulged a sneer at his expense. "Yea, I would rather lose my crown," said Richard, "than secure it by such means." "My cousin," James replied, "is too solicitous for the welfare of a nation that hesitates to acknowledge him as either a subject or a king."

4. An English army under Dacres was assembling in their front; an army which the clansmen could not meet in fight. A wasted country offered but a poor support to hungry men. Should they advance on Yorkshire, or retreat behind the Pentland hills? The Duke and Lady Catharine urged the King, their cousin, to advance. But James, who saw that Richard was no warrior, also saw that England would not rise. A woman called him to her bower at Stirling, and the flighty monarch wheeled about and fled. In hurrying through the Cheviot hills, a poorer, thirstier rabble than before, the clansmen shouted to the winds that some one had betrayed them to their English foes. Those men were wrong. Not one, but many, had betrayed them to their English foes. Half Stirling was in Henry's pay. The Bishop of Moray had agreed to help the English in repelling Richard, Duke of York. Buchan, a son of the Black Knight of Lorn, and Joan, Queen-widow of James the First, had taken service in the English court. Bothwell had asked for English gold. The Duke of Ross, a younger brother of the King, was on the English side, so far as such a boy could be on any side. A party in the court, aware of Henry's plans for a pacific union of the crowns, was bent on thwarting York. Some friends of Ross proposed to send him

to the English court. Buchan and Bothwell formed a plot to steal by night to the Pretender's camp, to seize his person as he lay asleep, and bear him to the nearest English town. In every quarter Richard and his wife had secret foes to watch and foil. They had no funds. They were indebted to the King of Scots for bread. They had no friends save such as youth and misery brought them. They were weak and human. Richard could not look on fire and blood without a wish to yield his claims, if giving up his rights would save the waste of life. His tenderness had weakened the invading force, disturbed his intercourse with James, and driven from him the Highland clans.

5. Of all his foes, the most adroit was Pedro de Ayala, envoy from the King of Spain. By marrying Lady Catharine, he had made Fernando the most deadly of his foes; for if he now succeeded in his claim, another Catharine would be Queen of England, and another family would supply a race of English kings. Since Henry had become a member of the League, it was Fernando's cue to stand by him; and Stirling having now become a nest of French intrigues, he chose to plant an agent in the Scottish court. This agent was a priest, a protonotary, and a man of family, who knew the world even better than he knew the Church. In dress, in manner, and in speech, Ayala was a contrast to the lame comedian at the English court. A gentleman of handsome person and engaging tongue, he found a way to every heart. He hired a goodly house; he kept a delicate table; and by scattering presents

to his right and left, he made a friend in almost every house. He noted Scot and Scotland with a cunning eye. By sparkling wit and pleasant ways, the Spanish proto-notary soon became a favourite of all parties in the Scottish capital; and that in spite of what they called, and very justly called, a recent insult to their King and state.

6. When Puebla had first come to London, he had been instructed to inquire about the Scots; what kind of men they were; what sort of land they lived in; how they could be turned to good account by Spain. Fernando's aims on England had compelled him to consider Scotland. Scotland was the friend of France. If Henry could be got to throw an army into Normandie, the Scots were sure to hurl their clans across the Tweed, and half the English forces would be wanted to repel these inroads on the northern shires. If Scotland could be made to keep the peace through Spanish means, Fernando would be still more powerful at the English court. So Puebla had been told to ask if James would wed Juana, daughter of Fernando by his Catalan mistress. He had imagined Scotland as a savage waste; but he had learned to his surprise that Scotland was a civilized kingdom, that her ruler was a poet and a soldier, that her peasantry were high in mood, and that her nobles were as ancient and as haughty as the dukes and counts of Spain. How could he name Fernando's offer of his Catalan daughter to the King of Scots? Not daring to propose that James should wed a bastard, he had dropt the question of Juana's birth, and let

the King of Scots imagine he was treating for a daughter of the King and Queen. A comedy of errors had been played for many months; a false Juana and a true Juana threading in and out; till James had heard from other quarters that the girl he talked of wedding was contracted to the son of Max. At once, he had inquired of Puebla, and the cripple, in reply to James, had reached the highest of his many flights. No doubt, he had replied to James, there was a new Juana in the field, who was to marry Philip, son of Max; but Philip was to wed the second, not the first; the first and best Juana had been kept for James. Both girls, he had assured the court, were daughters of Fernando; both were born in wedlock; both were heiresses of all his crowns. But James would have the elder-born. According to the canon's story, everything seemed clear. Before Fernando married Isabel, he had been married to the Catalan lady, and the princess, being the elder-born, might live to wear the crowns of Aragon, Sicily, Sardinia, and the whole of their dependent duchies. James had seized his offer, and appointed envoys to proceed to Spain, while Puebla, laughing in his cloak, had written joyously to say how thoroughly he had gulled the King of Scots.

7. Unhappily his masters had not read his letters in the proper light. They had their doubts whether James was such a fool as Puebla thought him. Puebla had said the Scots would be a little hot; but savage heat soon cools; and when their hands had touched the Spanish silver they would say no

more about the Catalan lady's birth. But how, the King and Queen had asked, could they prevent the truth being told? How, too, were they to be assured that James would pocket the affront? To them the lie had seemed a grave affair; and though they praised the cripple for his wit, they had not seen their way to make a profit by his falsehoods. "You have acted for the best," they had assured him, in reply to his disclosures; "yet it was not prudent to assert that Doña Juana is a legitimate daughter of Fernando. You should tell the truth before the Scotch ambassadors leave their country. Seeing by what roads they have to come, some one will surely tell them. Even we ourselves should have to tell the truth at last." If, when he understood this matter, James had been content to take the Catalan for a wife, they would have given her heaps of ducats; and as James was short of money, they had hoped he might go forward in the match. "Her dowry shall be doubled if the King will wed her." But they had not thought of giving him a daughter of the royal house. On Puebla hinting that they might do well to let him have Maria, they had said with brazen front, "If James expects to get a princess, you must put him off with lies. A plain refusal of his suit from us would drive him over to the French."

CHAPTER III.

Richard the Fourth.

1497.

1. SEVEN years had passed since this rebuff was given, yet James had never smoothed his brow towards Spain. Ayala had to clear the ground. He had to get this prince, the warmest friend of France, to look at men and things through Spanish eyes. It was no easy task, and yet the Spanish priest soon found a way to work. The King was low in mood; in part from failure in the war; in part from fear of Henry; and in part from a mishap in love. Ayala soothed and cheered him. An ambassador from a mighty prince, he spoke to James as though he were an Emperor; suggesting brides for him, as though a King of Scots could pick a wife from any family in the world. The King was young, with several amours on his hands. Ayala found one mistress in the palace, and another in a country house. Bonny Margaret Drummond was the reigning toast, but Lady Janet Kennedy disturbed her empire in the King. There had been many more. "The noble families," said Ayala, "favoured his intrigues in order to procure advantages for themselves." Ayala led him to renounce these evil courses, and to turn his thoughts towards marriage

with a lady of some royal house. Doña Maria, then at the Alhambra, Princess Margaret, then at Sheen, were held before his eyes as ladies of the highest birth, who might be asked to share his throne. James listened to a guest whose words made music in his veins. A match with Spain would fill his heart with pride; a match with England might result in giving his posterity the English crown.

2. At first, Ayala was not clear about his master's game. If he had given Maria to the King of Scots Berwick might have been to-day a border town, and Scotland might have been to England all that Portugal has been to Spain. But she could not be spared for Stirling. "Then, if James is not to have Maria," wrote Ayala, "he will turn his eyes towards Margaret." That was in Fernando's thoughts; and that was what Ayala was instructed to secure. "A truce, a peace, a marriage, and a crown," were the alluring prizes which Ayala was to dangle in the eyes of James, who soon began to see his duty with Ayala's eyes. If pride forbade him to desert a prince who had become a member of his house, his arm grew slacker in the cause with every turn of thought and every pause of speech. His rage for rushing through the Cheviots cooled. He listened to the men who spoke of peace, and though the Rose of York received from him the honours of a prince, sharp eyes could see amidst the cheer some signs that his affairs were hastening to their fall.

3. Ayala sailed for London with a secret man-

date from the King, his master, in his belt, appointing him ambassador at the English court, and noting him to Henry as a man of special trust. Fernando had resolved to bring about a truce between the English and the Scottish Kings, and even to prepare a union of the greater with the lesser crown. Ayala was the man for this pacific work. That Puebla would be jealous of their envoy was foreseen by Isabel, who tried to soothe him by a string of lies. Ayala was her minister to James, but not to Henry, she explained. His letters were a sham, and only to be shown in case he fell into some cruiser's snare. When he was safe on shore, he was to tear them up. But Puebla murmured, that this agent stayed in London, and was constantly in Henry's closet. She affected to be angry at Ayala having left his proper post, and threw the blame on Henry, who appeared, she said, to exercise a sort of fascination on the proto-notary. But Puebla was to carry on his business, as before Ayala came, and write to her in greater detail. When the cripple had been lulled by specious words, she sent two spies to London, with instructions to observe his ways of life, to see what place he held, and find out anything they could against him. Fray Johannes de Matienzo, sub-prior of Santa Cruz, and Sancho de Londoño, knight and soldier, were these spies.

4. Ayala was a man to take the eye and catch the ear of Henry; for his person and his purpose were exactly to the royal mind. A truce, a peace, and after peace a match, were what he wished to

bring about. Constructive in his genius, he had dreamed of that arrangement of the border strife, and once at least he had been ready with his treaty. When Ayala hinted that the swiftest way to crush the Rose of York was to arrange with James, he found the King familiar with his line of thought. Already, by his Welsh and Irish policy, he had taken some preliminary steps towards founding one great monarchy on British soil. The end was still far off; but he had partly cleared the ground, and shown the masons where to build. To found that monarchy, a reconciliation of the Welsh and a conciliation of the Irish were not all; the Scots must ome into the union; and a hundred years of war had proved to every man of sense that Scotland was a country never to be won by force of arms. Alliance might succeed. But how were they to move? It was for James to sue. The King of Scots denied his title, entertained a rival "king," and led his clans across the Tweed. Pride, anger, and revenge, the fiercest passions of the human heart, inflamed his border shires, and any treating with the Scots, except by sword and brand, might stir up swarms of foes whom he could ill afford to brave. Apart from passion, every one could see the value of a truce and match. Ayala knew the case of Portugal. If Spain could give her daughter to a Portuguese for peace, why should not England give her daughter to a Scot for peace?

5. Ayala was allowed to feel his way with James, but only if he spoke as working on ideas of

his own. On going back to Leith, he found his friend the King of Scots depressed in mind. A raid on Norham, which he fancied he could take asleep, was helping him to see his duties as Ayala saw them. Norham was a castle on the Tweed, then occupied by Bishop Fox. A few days' notice of the Scots' approach sufficed for Fox, who called-in men, and put his guns in order. When the clans came storming up the bank, he met them with a hail of shot that broke their companies into spray, and drove them down the steep in headlong rout. Much sobered by his check, the King began to treat of terms. "Surrender Perkin," said the Bishop. "Never!" answered James; "I am no judge of whether he be Duke of York or not; but I received him as a suppliant; I married him to my kinswoman; I believed he was a prince; and cannot sell him for my personal gain." The prudent bishop took what he could get. A truce was signed, and articles of peace were sketched; but Henry would not listen to a word so long as James consented to protect the Rose of York.

6. Ayala worked on James; and James, though much against his will, suggested to his guest, that, since the English would not rise in his behalf, and since the Scots had done their best for him, he would do well to seek some other home, and try his chances on some other coast. All forms of courtesy were still observed with him. His rank was recognised, his escort found, his table served, his pension paid; but he was told in many a sigh and gesture, that the time had come for him to

leave. If Lady Catharine chose to go with him, she should be free to go. The Scots believed in him, but they had done their utmost in his cause, and were not bound to waste their country for the House of York. A ship was fitted out for sea; some smaller barks were added for his men. His consort went on board with him; and in the midst of sad adieux, the youth whom every one in Scotland, from the King to his obscurest page, believed to be King Edward's son, set sail from Ayr.

It was Fernando's breath that drove him out.

CHAPTER IV.

More White Roses.

1497.

1. THE Rose of York and his adoring wife were not the only Roses to be clipt. Of Arthur's rivals, there was hardly one to whom, in other days, Fernando would have scrupled to transfer his child. A red Rose and a white Rose were to him the same; but he had now made up his mind to win on Henry's son. All other Roses, therefore, were but thorns and briers, to be removed as Carlos and Pacheco were removed. If Catharine sailed for England, she must come to share an undisputed throne. All rivals of the Prince of Wales must disappear.

2. The first in blood was Edward, Earl of Warwick, son of George, the murdered Duke of Clarence. Cousin to the Queen, he stood behind her and her sisters in the legal order; but the right of females to succeed in person was denied in fact, if not in law; and after Catharine Gordon's husband, all the Yorkists looked on Edward as their rightful prince. A weak and inoffensive youth, his name alone was dangerous to the King; a soldier with no sounder title than a battle won by mercenary bands; but he was saved from hurting any one, and most of all from injuring himself. He was a prisoner in the Tower. When Simnel rose in Dublin,

and announced himself as Edward, Earl of Warwick, Henry had put the true Plantagenet under guard, and as the times grew perilous, had prepared for him a lodging in the pile so fatal to his race. The partizans of Simnel called the prisoner an impostor; and these partizans of Simnel are not yet extinct. Ten years he had been kept in durance. Happier than his father and his cousin, Edward, last male prince of the Plantagenets, was "forgotten" in the Tower.

3. The next in blood came Edmond, Earl of Suffolk, son of Lady Bessie, eldest sister of King Edward and King Richard. Lady Bessie had married John de la Pole, second Duke of Suffolk, to whom she had borne five sons and four daughters; all of whom stood high in favour with their uncle Richard, and were placed by him in close succession to the crown. A violent age and an unsettled law had given the reigning prince a voice in choosing who should follow him; and Richard, on his son's demise, had fixed on John de la Pole, his sister's eldest son, as heir-presumptive to the throne. No other choice was left. The son of Clarence stood before him, but the son of Clarence was attainted by his father's crime. The daughters of King Edward had been set aside. John de la Pole was next in blood, and being a dashing soldier, seemed the fittest prince to carry on the line of York. The highest post in Richard's gift, the Lord Lieutenancy of Ireland, had been conferred on him. Nor had his younger brothers been forgotten. Humphrey, having taken orders, had been made a

prebendary of St. Paul's, and Edward, having also taken orders, an Archdeacon of Richmond, in the diocese of York. These rich and stately posts were but the steps by which they were to reach the pastoral staff and cardinal's hat. His sister, Lady Anne, had been engaged to James, the heir-apparent of the King of Scots. Had fortune turned against the mercenary bands at Bosworth, John de la Pole and Lady Anne would have worn the English and the Scottish crowns. That battle had destroyed the House of Pole.

4. By bending to the storm, the Duke had saved some portion of a mighty wreck. A thrifty son of thrifty Yorkshire fathers, Pole had trimmed his sail and got his bark to port; and having in his veins no royal blood, had been allowed to keep his money and his ducal rank. But the Plantagenet yeast being strong within his sons, they could not brook their fall from princely state and regal hope. The King had been disposed to treat them kindly. He had called them to his councils, and was willing to regard them as a younger branch. But John, so lately heir, was rash and restless, and while courting Henry's smiles, had entered into plots against his crown and life. Afraid of fortune, he had fled to Flanders, where his aunt, the Duchess Margaret, gave him shelter, till he crossed the sea to Ireland, where he still affected to be Lord Lieutenant, though that office had been given by Henry to his uncle Jasper. Pole had sworn that Simnel was his cousin Edward, Earl of Warwick, the legitimate heir of Richard's crown. In Simnel's service he had landed, fought, and fallen.

5. Attainders having swept away the family estate, his younger brother, Edmond, was too poor to hold his rank as duke, and had to sell his patent to the crown. The King bestowed on him the rank of earl, and strove to win him over to his side. Pacific and inventive, it was Henry's care to live in peace with all the Yorkist princes, if the Yorkist princes would accept him as their king. He lost in many ways by lodging Warwick in the Tower; and Edmond de la Pole at court, in seeming favour, was a sign that Henry had some cause beyond the jealousy of a rival prince, for keeping Warwick under watch and ward. Young Pole was near the King, and treated as a cousin by the Prince of Wales. When Henry was created Duke of York, his cousin Pole was foremost in the feast and dance, and took from Queen Elizabeth's hands a handsome ring. Desiring all the world to note how much he trusted Pole, the King went down to his house in Ewelme, near Wallingford, where he deigned to sleep beneath his rival's roof. Yet Pole was very bitter in his heart against the King. His loss of rank and fortune galled him. He had fallen in the world; not only far below his birth, but even below his father's birth. The Poles had held the rank of Duke and Marquis fifty years; yet he, whose mother was a princess of the blood, must walk behind my Lord of Bucks! Young, rash, and false, Pole needed to be watched by curious eyes, and kept in bounds by many unseen hands.

6. From Ayr the Rose of York stood over for the Irish coast, where he imagined every knight and kerne would rise on his approach. But Ireland was

CHAP. IV.—MORE WHITE ROSES. 1497.

no longer what she had been in her lawless days. The reins were held in English hands; the team was driven with English strength. Repelled from port to port, the fugitive found no inch of ground on which to set his feet. He knocked at many gates, and found no entrance till he sighted County Cork. John Walters and the citizens of Cork were staunch, but in the higher regions every one seemed changed. By clemency and humour Henry had begun to win upon the Irish fancy. Poynings had repaired to London, leaving Father Henry in his post, and Father Henry had in turn retired in favour of Kildare. An Anglo-Irish chief was ruling Dublin, and an English lady, cousin to the King, was governing that Anglo-Irish chief. Kildare having now become a loyal officer, his kith and kin were suitors to the Countess of Kildare for place and pay. Even Desmond, rallying for the King, rode down to Cork, and tried to snare the man for whom he had so lately risked his head. A fleet ran out from Waterford, which city had not yet forgiven the fugitive, and anchored in the Cove of Cork. As foes were coming up by sea and land, the titular Duke and Duchess stood in peril of their lives, until the faithful Walters counselled them to fly while any road lay open for escape. At dead of night, he and his son put them in a skiff, fell down the river Lee, and passing through the ships at anchor, sailed with them for a deserted rock called Leprous Island, lying off the headland of Kinsale.

CHAPTER V.

Clearing the Ground.

1497-9.

1. WHAT port was open to the fugitives from Cork? What mayor would follow them like Walters? Philip had become so cool, they could not venture on a Flemish harbour. France was closed to them by Charles. They dared not land in Spain; and Venice was too far away. Nor could they rest on Leprous Island, for an English fleet was on their track. In something like despair, they listened to a voice from Cornwall, where the Celtic commons had been lately in a discontented mood. A Spanish bark was at their service, for the Spanish skippers gave their ready help to any Rose of York. With ninety men on board this Spanish bark, they sailed for Whitesand Bay, and threw themselves on shore. "Rake-hell," cried Henry, when he heard the news, "has landed in the west!" A fleet was instantly despatched to Whitesand Bay. "We have the knave at last." A tailor and a smith who joined the Duke of York, informed him how the Cornish men had lately marched to London Bridge, how they had found the King despised, how no man raised a lance for him, till they were near the Thames. They had no general, and they had to turn, the tailor added; but the King, although he got the better

of them in a push of pikes, had hardly dared to press them in retreat. That King was offering them his pardon, but the Cornish men despised him and his gifts. Give them a general and they undertook to crown his rival in a month. The fugitive listened, like a man in desperate fortune, to these foolish tales. Still unaware that he was not a soldier, he secured his consort in St. Michael's Mount, and marching with the tailor and the smith, he reached the town of Bodmin, where a rabble from the mines and hedges came into his camp and hailed him as their king.

2. "Who serves me now," said Henry, more in look than words, "even though he come in at the eleventh hour, will earn the wages of a day." A host of men sprang up to serve him; for the blindest partizan of York could see that, whether "Rake-hell" were Plantagenet or Perkin, he could never more escape. Daubeney marched into the west. The Courtneys and Carews were soon afield. Brooke leapt to horse, and Buckingham put on his mail. A hundred friars went out to help their patron with the spiritual arm. Except that Celtic rabble from the mines and hedges, no one joined the Rose of York; and that poor rabble, in and out of whom a band of friars kept passing, soon began to melt away. A rumour ran among them that the New-Year's grain and ale were cursed, and all who ate and drank of them were dying in their sins. It was remembered how the Church had censured those who lately marched against the King; the men, the fields, the crops, the granaries; and lo, the corn

and malt had all been turned to poison by the wrath of God! Too surely, they were fighting in an unblest cause. They might be stiff in heart and stout in limb, but who was strong enough to wrestle with the unseen powers?

3. Before Daubeney's troops could reach them, they had summoned Exeter to yield, and finding more resistance than a mob could overcome, had turned off north towards Taunton, where the soldiers coming from all quarters of the compass caught them in a belt of steel. The Cornish men were hot for fight, but York grew faint of heart as Daubeney drew nigh. "A sanctuary!" cried the luckless youth; "I cannot stay and see my people slain." He rode to Bewley Abbey, a Cistercian cloister in the New Forest, where the abbot gave him shelter, till the offer of a pardon from the King induced him to come out. No force was needed, for the Church was on the regal side, and rights of sanctuary could be either lengthened or abridged by Rome. The King appeared to speak him fair. His wife, already captured in the west, was at the royal mercy; and the hapless Rose of York had reason to believe that if he yielded his pretensions to the crown, his life and honour would be safe.

4. The fight was done, and could not be renewed. What matter whether he were prince or commoner? By giving up his regal claim, he might regain his freedom and recover the companionship of his wife. On yielding, he would have to own the fraud. But if the King might call him Osbek, he was likely to forgive the rest. The Mayor of

Cork and his devoted son were prisoners, and the lives of these true servants hung upon his lips. On saying he was "Osbek," he was kindly greeted by the King, who sent for Lady Catharine to his court. The pair were lodged in Henry's house. To Lady Catharine he was kind, for Lady Catharine was not only young and beautiful, but was a cousin of the King of Scots. To keep her from her lord, without appearing to be harsh, he sent her with a message to the Queen, in whose apartments she remained— a royal guest and hostage for her cousin James. "This youth," the shrewd Raimondo wrote, "has vanished into smoke."

5. Ayala seized the hour of victory to urge his scheme of union. Morton gave him help. Those bishops who were oftenest in Henry's closet, Richard Fox and William Smyth, were warm supporters of a Scottish marriage. William Warham, Master of the Rolls, a man of higher reach than either Fox or Smyth, and oftener in the privy chamber, also pressed the match. Assured of strong support at Sheen, the Spanish proto-notary rode to Stirling. James had ceased his raids, and every one was anxious to discuss the English terms. Ayala's object was a secret, and a secret kept so well that even the wily agents of the Signory, who learned that he had some commission from the English King, inferred that he was sent to bring about a match between the Scotch and Spanish courts. James liked Ayala's plan so well, that he appointed him commissioner to the English King; and thus a stranger in the land was actually made ambassador

from James to Henry and from Henry to James. A truce was signed, and something better than a truce prepared.

6. Fernando's plans seemed ripening fast, but still those rival Roses were unclipped. A pair of youthful and mysterious guests at court, who were received and lodged like princes, caused Fernando some misgivings. Lady Catharine in the Queen's apartments, always near her person, seemed to him suspicious. Save that "Osbek" only saw his wife in presence of other parties, he was not restrained. But soon a change came over his affairs. The thought of an escape was put into his head. The road seemed open, if he chose to go. He quitted London in disguise, and was arrested in the act of flight. This flight was given in evidence of a plot against the King. Condemned to public shame, the youth was fastened in a pillory, and when he had been hooted, pitied, and abused, according to the humours of a crowd, he was conveyed into the Tower for safety. From his chamber to a coffin was a step. Beside him in his prison lay that hapless Edward, son of Clarence, who had been "forgotten" in the Tower. The keepers let the young men see each other and engage in foolish talk. They were accused of plotting to escape; were tried, condemned, and sentenced to be put to death! Could such a sentence be enforced? With "Osbek" there was little pause. Stern judges, treating him as an alien, ordered him to be hung on Tyburn tree. He had a promise of his life; but needs of state compelled the council to enforce the law. John Walters

and his son, both true to him in life and death, were judged to share his fate. All three were taken in a cart to the accursed spot and hung.

7. With Edward, Earl of Warwick, there was longer pause. Plantagenet had never been in arms; had never claimed the crown; had never plotted to upset the King. An effort to escape from prison was not treason. But the King and Queen of Spain were thirsting for his blood. Plantagenet was to them another Excellenta; and their daughter Catharine could not mount a menaced throne. Few words were said on either side. The times were harsh, and men were used to tragic woes; but secret poisoning was a crime from which the English soul recoiled. Some letters out of Spain were shown, from which the council gathered that the prince must die. Ten months elapsed; but in the last days of November writs were issued for his execution; and a prince of the blood, a prisoner from his youth, was taken from his cell, and hacked to death, in order that Infanta Catalina might not find a rival near her husband's crown. "The King," as Bacon says, "did not observe that he did bring a kind of malediction on the marriage." Yet the fact was so, "The Lady Catharine herself," the writer adds, "a sad and religious woman, long after, when King Henry the Eighth's resolution of a divorce from her was first made known to her, used some words that she had not offended, but it was a judgment of God, for that her former marriage was made in blood; meaning that of the Earl of Warwick."

It was Fernando's axe that clove his neck.

CHAPTER VI.

A House of Woe.

1500-1.

1. But while the rope and axe were clearing ground in England for the Princess Catharine to come in, the curse invoked by Hebrew bard and Moorish knight was working in her mother's house in Spain. Don Juan, sickening in his honeymoon, was dead. Too suddenly his soul had filled with Marguerite's light and life. That lady, followed into Spain by crowds of poets, cavaliers, and artists, seemed to have no other care than studying how to make her day one round of festive grace. Her joyous spirits were too high for the reserved and silent youth, whose years had passed in convents, with a secretary of the Inquisition by his side. "Let them be parted for a time," his leeches said. "No, no," groaned Isabel; "whom God has joined let no man put asunder." And the prince had faded from her sight. At Salamanca, fever seized upon his feeble frame. By riding hard, Fernando was in time to see him die, but Isabel had never seen his face again. At nineteen years of age, this heir of twenty crowns was laid in that especial home of the Dominicans, the convent of Santo Tomas, near Avila, which his mother had erected with a

portion of the money she had wrung from Moors and Jews. His widow bore a son, but when this heir of Spain was born, to Isabel's despair the child was dead.

2. Juan and his son being gone, the "curse of Portugal" stood next in order of succession, and her husband thought he saw within his grasp the diadems for which he had forgotten John's remorse and multiplied the Excellenta's wrongs. The King and Queen of Portugal crossed the frontier into Spain, in order to receive the oaths of fealty, and in other ways secure their future rights. In Seville and the conquered lands they met with no rebuff. Castille, an old and liberal country, made conditions. Aragon, an older and more liberal country, raised the constitutional question as to whether females could succeed. It was a mooted point, and Isabel began to fear that after all her crimes, and after all Fernando's crimes, the union of Castille and Aragon was insecure. If members of the Cortes could dispute her children's birthright while Fernando lived, what would they fear to do when he was dead? She said, in her alarm, it would be better to have done with parley, to dismiss the Cortes, to annul the fundamental pact, and to subdue the country as Granada was subdued. Appeal to codes and rules enraged her, and she longed to hold the kingdom as she held the Caliphate, by force of arms. But even in the Aljaferia she heard a warning voice. "We stand upon our oaths, we men of Aragon," replied Antonio de Fonseca; "we must look before we leap; for what you ask of us is hard to justify

according to our usages and laws." Worse things than legal questions in the Casa Blanca and disloyal speeches in the Aljaferia were behind. In truth, the kindred of the murdered Friends of Light might well have found some pity for their Queen. While she was wrangling with the deputies over points of law, the object of her care fell sick. Forebodings seized the Child of Sin. She felt and said she was about to die. No bustle at the Aljaferia could rouse her spirits, and in giving birth to her first child she died.

3. Miguel, her orphan son, was heir of Portugal and Spain, of Sicily, Sardinia, part of Naples, both the Indies, and the rest of their dependent states. Though he had lost his consort, Manoel seemed to have secured the object of his reign. A son of his was heir of all the kingdoms from the Straits of Messina to the outer ocean. But the vials were not spent, as yet. Don Miguel withered in his crib and died.

4. Juana, wife of Philip the Fair, was now the heiress, and her infant Carl, an Austrian prince, stood next in order of succession to the King and Queen. The Catholic kingdoms were to pass into a foreign house, and Catholic Spain would know her native kings no more. Nor was the bitter draught commended to their lips by any grace on Philip's part. That Austrian would not wait for Miguel's death before he took the style of Prince of Castille. Already his pretensions were unbearable. Juana, too, was growing every year more liberal. She refused to house her mother's spies. She would

CHAP. VI.—A HOUSE OF WOE. 1500-1.

not take a Spanish friar from Santa Cruz for her confessor. She declined to live, as Isabel had lived, according to monastic rules. A son of Kaiser Max, the Archduke added to a winsome face a flighty temper and a calculating brain. He was in daily want of coin, and spent his fretful hours in counting up the ducats he would have as King of Spain. He asked the King and Queen for money, power, and recognition. If the King and Queen were slow in granting his requests, he stormed against them and reproached his wife. She was in love with Philip, and she strove to satisfy him, even at her father's cost. Fernando was beginning to regard his son-in-law and daughter with a cold and dangerous kind of fear.

5. Would Manoel now remember John's advice, and seek to vindicate the royal maid? Fernando had two daughters at Granada. That Maria whom the King of Portugal had once rejected, was become, in consequence of all these deaths, a prize. She stood the next in order to Juana. Should Juana's offspring fail, Maria would be Queen of Spain. When Manoel had laid her sister in the grave he sent proposals for her hand. If his proposals for the elder sister had been treated as a scandal, these advances to Maria seemed no less than infamous. Maria was related to him in the first degree, and marriage in the first degree is contrary to a code which neither pope nor council can suspend. But Isabel had to ask herself the question — what if Manoel were refused? The Excellenta was at Santa Clara; and if Manoel were to marry her, he

could throw the country into civil strife. She feared, and had good cause to fear, the chances of a civil war. The whole resources of her realm were taxed. From Sicily and Naples came a daily cry for men, more men. A rising had occurred among the workmen of Granada, which was hardly quelled before a general insurrection broke along the mountain ridges, from the Alpujarras almost to Europa Point. Her armies were so hardly pressed, that she was forced to yield whatever Portugal might choose to ask. A treaty therefore was arranged at the Alhambra, and Maria was conducted to her sister's throne.

6. These risings of the Moors, provoked by shameless violation of the articles of surrender, proved how little had been done towards conquering the conquered race. For weeks the rebels held a quarter of the capital. For weeks they menaced the Alhambra. They were only got to lay aside their arms by promises that every article of the treaty should be put in force, and every cause of discontent be done away. Ximenes would not keep these promises; and being backed by Isabel, he was converting the disarmed Mohammedans by force. A wail of woe went up from the great city; but the garrison was strong and ready, and Gonsalvo de Cordova was at his post. The gates were closed; the walls and towers were manned; and though the craftsmen chafed, they could not drive the garrisons from these walls and towers. But in the open country, where the garrisons were thin, the people flew to arms and leapt to horse. A dozen fortresses

were captured in a week. Gonsalvo marched against them, and at Huescar showed the world what Christian knights could do, by giving up the town to sack, by putting nearly all the men to death, and selling all the rest, together with their wives, for slaves. The rising spread. Fernando had to take the field; and by his sleepless energy had barely pacified the Alpujarras when a still more threatening movement called him to the west. Among the dales and passes of the Red Sierras rising east of Ronda, dwelt a race of warlike Moors, whose rage the King and Queen had striven to calm by promises of strict adherence to the terms of peace. Deceived a dozen times, these mountaineers unfurled their ancient flag. Alonzo, elder brother of Gonsalvo, led an army to the Red Sierras, where the Moors entrapped them in an ambuscade, and routed them with fearful loss. Alonzo was among the slain. So great a victory sent thrills of terror through the Christian camps. It seemed as if all Islam were about to rise; and should the Sultan carry out his threat, and send an army into Spain, the Caliphs might regain their palace on the hill. Disgusted with the Cardinal, whose breach of faith had caused this loss, the King exclaimed to Isabel, "Your priest has cost us dear; in a few hours he has thrown away the conquests of our lives." Again Fernando had to call on everyone for help, and ride away to Ronda, where his troops were gathering in their quarters for a hug of death.

7. The Queen was reeling in her mind. So many graves about her feet, so many ghosts about

her bed, so many troubles in her states, were more than mortal frame could bear. Confession ceased to bring her comfort. Acts of Faith no longer roused her spirits. The husband of her youth was causing her the keenest pangs. The two Juanas, one her niece and one her child, were always in her brain. She knew how much the great religious orders feared their future Queen. They had begun to slander her as they had done Enrique's child. If they could hardly touch her birth, they could attack her views. They said she was unsound of faith, and hinted that a girl unsound of faith must also be unsound of mind. With all her dead about her feet, and fretted by the vision of a truant husband and a disobedient child, the Queen was lonelier in her purple hall at the Alhambra than that niece in Santa Clara whom her acts had buried in a foreign cell.

8. Alone in her secluded chamber, Catharine waited for a signal to depart. Arrangements had been made to celebrate her nuptials in the previous fall. The English King had written to express his joy. A challenge had arrived from English peers and knights to break a lance with any gentlemen of Spain in honour of the match. The Cardinal of England had assumed a special patronage of her union. Arthur had sent his love, expressing his desire to see her, in a pretty note which Padre Alessandro could translate. The King, by crossing to his town of Calais in a time of sickness, made the personal acquaintance of her sister, the Archduchess, whose exceeding beauty won his eye and

CHAP. VI.—A HOUSE OF WOE. 1500-1.

heart. At Christmas she had ratified the contracts and espousals made for her by Puebla. Yet the King, her father, would not let her go. There was another prince to fear, another Rose of York to clip and cast away. Plantagenet being gone, the Yorkist party had begun to turn their eyes towards Edmond de la Pole; and then the council saw, a day too late, that in their eagerness to satisfy Fernando they had killed a fawn and put a leopard in his place. With a Plantagenet living, Edmond de la Pole had felt secure; but when the last Plantagenet was slain, he was himself the head of all offence. As next male heir of York, his life was in an enemy's hand. An agent of the Kaiser tempted him to fly by offers of support; and after supping with some Yorkist peers, and planning an invasion of the realm, Pole slipt away in secret, crossed the sea, and hurried to the court of Max.

CHAPTER VII.

A veiled Infanta.

1501.

1. EARLY on a bright October afternoon, a lady, veiled from crown to slipper, stept on shore at Plymouth from a Spanish ship. A crowd of barks were tossing in the Sound, and every tower and steeple were ablaze with flags. Some parts of what had been a Spanish fleet were riding near the Hoe, with prelates, counts, and dames on deck, and money, plates, and precious stones on board. The counts and dames were worn and white, and all seemed glad to set their feet on land. A church which stood beside the mole invited them to enter, and a priest being ready to begin his mass, the language common to all services of the church soon made these strangers feel at home. The lady veiled from crown to shoe was Catharine, that sister of the Order of St. Francis who for thirteen years had been the titular Princess of Wales.

2. She caught the first soft outline of the western coast on an autumnal day, when she was worn by fasting, sickness, and a stormy voyage, as weak in frame as she was galled in mind. Her parting from her parents had been strange. Her father was away at Ronda, and her mother was too sad and broken to escort her to the coast. Her home had been

a house of dole; and when she quitted the Alhambra she had started on her voyage alone. "She would be longer on the road," said Isabel, who could only travel with an army of confessors, nuns, and clerks. Her motive was to save expense. If Catharine was alone, she might be lodged in wretched villages and still more wretched inns. Aware how strong the contrast might be when her daughter landed on the English coast, for she had heard that every one was getting ready to receive her, Isabel begged the sovereign not to make too much of Catharine, and not to spend his money on a foolish show. She parted from her child, whose face she was to see no more, at the Alhambra. Catharine lodged in wayside inns; she prayed before the shrine of Santiago; she increased her train as she approached the coast; and having put to sea, was blown by tempests round Cape Ortegal, along the shores of the Asturias, and was driven for shelter into that small harbour of Laredo, where the English envoys who had come to seek her had been forced to land. Her sufferings were so great, she feared to face the sea again. Her ships were small and slight; her captain was a novice in his trade. All England had been roused by tales of her adventures, and the ablest sailor in the navy, Stephen Brett, had gone to meet her and conduct her little fleet to port.

3. When Catharine caught the welcome outline of her future home—the soft green sweep of down, the fine white front of cliff, the red and sparkling cove, on all of which a temperate sunshine lay—

her heart grew strong within her breast. A few
hours later, when she rode along the mole, her ear
drank in the hail and shout of those who lined the
beach, and then she made a vow that, come to her
what might of either good or ill, she never would
go back to Spain, as Isabel her sister had returned
from Portugal, with broken heart. These cheers
put life into her whitening cheek. Already she had
heard in Spain that England was a merry isle.
Already she had heard that lords and knights would
come to meet her; that the Round Table would be
spread again; and that a chapter of two hundred
and thirty knights would be revived in honour of
her husband and herself. But she had hardly
dreamt of such a welcome as she found. Her name,
her rosy cheek, her light blue eye, reminded people
of her English blood. Old love and hate found
voice in these warm plaudits from the western
shores. In Yorkist eyes she was an English princess, and a princess with a clearer title than the
King. A daughter of the land, she came to be
the mother of a race of kings. "The Princess,"
wrote Alcares to his royal mistress, "could not have
been received with greater joy, if she had been the
Saviour of the world."

4. The ship in which she came was laden with
her plates and jewels, and was crowded with the
servants of her household, and the magnates who
had come to see her dowry paid. Elvira Manuel,
a sister of the minister, Don Juan Manuel, then at
Bruges, had been appointed by the Queen her
"deputy." Elvira's actual rank was that of first

lady of honour and first lady of the bed-chamber; but she was to stand towards Catharine as a mother, and to see that no one raised her veil and looked upon her face until her nuptial day. Elvira's husband, Don Pedro Manrique, was first chamberlain and mayor of the palace. Don Inigo, her son, was master of the ceremonies and master of the pages. Juan de Cuero and his wife were master and mistress of the state rooms; but Cuero's foremost duty was to keep the royal plate. Alonzo de Esquivel, Knight commander, was her master of the hall. Maria de Rojas, Francisca de Silva, Beatrix de Blanca, and Martina de Salazar, were her maids of honour. Maria de Rojas was a daughter of Fernando's ablest foreign minister, and was herself as proud and able as her sire. In waiting on these ladies were two female slaves; no doubt, two Moorish maidens from Granada, who had been a part of Isabel's spoil. The Padre Alessandro was her first chaplain and confessor. An almoner, a secretary, a cup-bearer, a marshal, a chief butler, a warder of the chapel, four equerries, three gentlemen-in-waiting, a comptroller, a keeper of the plate, a cook, a quarter-master, a clerk of the stores, and purser followed. There was still a tail behind; including such small officers as a washerwoman, a waiter, and a sweep. Among the persons who attended as a train of honour, were Alonzo de Fonseca, Archbishop of Santiago, who was still engaged with the affair of Alcala, and Count de Cabra, one of the heroes of the Moorish war. These eminent persons were commissioners for the dowry, which they were to pay on seeing the bridal rites performed and getting evidence that the marriage was complete.

5. A crowd of knights and ladies from the western shires came riding into Plymouth to receive the Princess, bringing with them gifts and services, and forming on the spot a circle like a court. She stayed in Plymouth till her dowry, plate, and stuff were landed, and while messengers sped forward to announce her coming to the King. A little rest and some good dinners set her up; but the provincial knights and dames were puzzled by Elvira holding to the rule that Catharine must not lift her veil and show her face. Ayala, who had stayed in London by the King's desire, pretending to be waiting her arrival, but in secret busy with the Scottish peace and marriage, came to join her, and assume the main direction of her house; but he had no authority to break a rule laid down by Isabel, and Catharine wore her veil in public like a Moorish bride.

6. Willoughby de Brooke spurred down into the west, attended by Red Dragon, Mont Orgueil, and Richmond King-at-Arms, to meet her grace at Exeter, to ride before her through the counties, and to furnish her with horses, carriages, and lodgings on the road. On quitting Exeter, she supped and slept at Honiton, Crewkerne, Sherborne, Shaftesbury; lodging in the abbey when there was an abbey, in the parsonage when there was a parsonage, and in the absence of either parsonage or abbey at an inn. Two miles from Amesbury, on the Avon, she was

met by Thomas Earl of Surrey, Lord High Treasurer, and his wife. Surrey's wife, Elizabeth, who held the titular rank of Duchess of Norfolk, was appointed mistress of the household. Surrey was attended by two prelates, two mitred abbots, two barons, and six knights, who carried her in state to Amesbury, where she dined and slept. No words could pass between her English escort and her Spanish servants; but the titular Duchess had a man named Hollybrand in her train who spoke Castillian, and by means of Hollybrand some words of welcome were conveyed from Surrey and his wife to Catharine in her native tongue. On every side the princess saw what pains were taken for her comfort; pains so striking when compared against the freezing farewells of her kith and kin. In sending her a welcome to his country, Henry begged of her to love and trust him in the days to come, and look upon his country as her own. He told her he was coming with her prince, Arthur of Winchester, who, like the King himself, was said to be on fire till he could look upon her face.

7. Fonseca and Elvira said this license could not be allowed. What! look upon the maiden's face? Their orders were to hide her like a Moorish bride. Fernando was so sure that Henry would attempt to cheat him, that he laid two "strict injunctions and commands" on the Archbishop of Santiago; first, that he was not to pay one ducat of Catharine's dowry till the marriage-rites had been performed; and next, that he was not to suffer either king or prince to see her till the bridegroom had obtained a right to draw aside her veil in church.

CHAPTER VIII.

First Interview.

1501.

1. How could a man who trusted neither wife nor child, put faith in such a schemer as the Tudor prince, whom he had found a mate in guile, and feared to find a match in fraud? The English King might still cry off, propose another wife for Arthur, and retain his daughter Catharine as a pledge. Suppose the Prince, himself a comely boy, should see no beauty in his Spanish bride? All English eyes were spoiled. The Queen was perfect in her charms; her court was full of lovely maids; in every park and street a man might see such faces as recalled his peerless Queen. Nor was Fernando's daughter fairest of her train. The English King had seen her sister, and might fancy Catalina was a younger version of Juana. As an artist and a worshipper of beauty, Henry had requested that no plain maid of honour should be sent with Catharine. Gentle birth was much, but youth and comeliness were more. If they were beautiful, these damsels might attract adorers; and by marrying in the country they would live in Catharine's sight. The loveliest damsels had been chosen as companions of her voyage, and in the light of their exceeding beauty

she might seem to Arthur flat and dull. Suppose the Prince refused to have her? How could Spain compel him? Contracts were but words. There was the rite at Bewdley Manor, where the Prince had pledged his troth; but here Fernando felt no safer than he felt on secular ground. Grave doubts existed as to whether that solemnity was lawful. It was secret, and the Church forbade clandestine marriages. Smyth, Bishop of Lincoln, who performed the rite, had stated in the chapel that the ceremony was irregular, and asked a secular peer to read the contract in his place. A prelate, he incurred the danger of suspension from his office if he read the service. Puebla had been forced to interfere. As papal agent, he declared the Pope's approval of that secret rite. Nay, more, the King of England and the Queen of Spain required it. What had Smyth to fear? Smyth answered that he had his doubts; and Puebla, who could see how easily these doubts might touch his mistress in the future, sent a full account of what the Bishop had observed to Spain. Fernando meant to run no risk, to put no hostage in a rival's hand, to have no child sent back to him in shame, and so his orders had been given that Catharine's veil should not be lifted by the Prince until they met in church.

2. But how could the Archbishop and dueña carry out this rule? A king is master of his house. On English soil Fernando had no voice, except so far as Henry might allow. If either King or Prince should meet them on the road, and ask to see the bride, what man would dare to answer that he

should not lift her veil? As neither King nor Prince was yet aware of these commands being laid, Ayala, knowing how a Tudor would receive such news, felt anxious to avoid a scene. The King should be informed. If they could reach him in the outset of his journey, he might turn aside and wait for them at Sheen. All wrangles would be spared, and Catharine's face might still be veiled from English eyes. At Dogmersfield, in Hants, the house of Oliver, Bishop of Bath and Wells, the Spaniards heard that Henry and his son were on the road. At once it was proposed to warn them; and Ayala, as a man who knew them well, rode forward towards East Hampstead, which the King and Prince had lately left. If any messenger could have stopped the King, Ayala was the man. Not many weeks had passed since Henry had requested him to wait in England till the Princess came. No man knew more of Henry's mind than he; no man was busier with the royal hopes than he; but Henry was a prince not easily turned aside.

3. Two miles from Dogmersfield, Ayala met the royal party riding towards the Bishop's house. The King and Prince were ambling like two knights in front, with prelates, peers, and cavaliers behind them. "Stay, your highness," cried Ayala. Henry reined his horse, and listened to the proto-notary. They must go as they had come. The lady Catharine was at Dogmersfield; her Spanish servants were about her; and by order of Ayala's master, Catharine could receive no visit, see no company, until the morning of her nuptial rites. The King

sat musing in his saddle, as his mythic Hero might have sat and mused. The boy who bore that Hero's name was at his side. Behind him rode the prelates, earls, and councillors, who helped him to conduct his realm, and far as eye could reach the road was all agog with pages, knights, and men-at-arms. Before him sat Ayala, in his hood and gown, forbidding him, in his own realm, to see a lady who was called by every tongue Princess of Wales. By order of the King of Spain! What could Fernando mean? He called a council on the spot—the spot an open meadow on the road from Winchfield; when he told his barons what Ayala said, and asked them whether, in his proper kingdom, Catharine could be hidden from his sight, and that of her contracted groom? The temporal and spiritual peers made answer with one voice that, since the lady was on English soil, she was protected by the English law. These Spanish servants had no power to shut her doors; and Henry, as the lord of all, might see her when and how he pleased.

4. "Then follow," cried the King, and, striking spurs into his horse, he rode to Dogmersfield, and ere the Spanish servants knew what message had been given, he was within the Bishop's gates. In boots and belt, with sword and cloak, he pushed his way into the house. What page or abigail could stay his foot? The Count de Cabra put himself in front, but Henry passed the hero of Lucena as he might have done the youngest page. Fonseca, counting on his clerical habit, tried to bar his way. "She is retired within her room, your highness," he

began. "I will see and speak with her," said Henry, "even if she were gone to bed." Fonseca had to go and tell his mistress that the King was come and would not be denied. She seemed to like this greeting well, and walked into an outer chamber, called the third, where she was told he was. He spoke to her in French, and was amused and grieved to find that she had still that tongue to learn. She spoke no language save Castillian. She observed that Henry's tones were sweet, for he was gentle with the child, whose honest face, blue eyes, and sunny hair were pleasant in his sight.

5. Too young to ride as Henry rode, the Prince came after him, all slushed and soiled with the November rain; and, after washing hands and changing clothes, he joined his father, who conducted him to the second chamber, where the Prince and Princess saw each other face to face. The scene was quaint and droll. They bowed and kissed. Each held the other's palm, and spoke his love, the boy in English and the girl in Spanish. Councillors and bishops stood about. When Arthur told his bride he loved her well, a bishop turned his phrases into Latin, which he whispered to a Spanish priest, who turned his love into Castillian. Henry put their hands into each other's, when he bade them pledge their mutual troth. Camelot sighed and Aragon smiled, and love was chiefly made through two young pairs of eyes. When supper, which they ate apart, was done, the King and Prince walked back to Catharine's room—the inner room this time—and there, in spite of all Fonseca had to

urge about his rule, they stayed till late at night. Elvira frowned, as a dueña should do. Cabra made his silent protest, for the hero was a knight who kept his word. But if her ladies stared at these free English manners, Catharine liked her guests, and, sending for musicians, she began to dance. If Arthur was too shy to lead her out, he danced a figure with his governess, Lady Guilford. Catharine's southern dances would be new to King and Prince, and Catharine tripped and twirled till Henry rose.

CHAPTER IX.

Days of Courtship.

1501.

1. NEXT day the King rode back to Sheen, the name of which he changed to Richmond, where he told the Queen of his adventures on the road; his meeting with Ayala in the fields; his pricking on to find the Princess; his encounter with her protonotary; and his amusing evening spent in Catharine's room. He added that he liked her person and her manner, and that Arthur was enchanted with his future bride.

2. Not only as a mother who desired the welfare of her son, but as a woman who had suffered in her youth, Elizabeth felt cheered. For peace, she thought, depended on the birth of heirs. As yet, she had to lean on two lives mainly; Arthur, Prince of Wales, and Henry, Duke of York. Her daughters weighed but little in the scale. Of course their rights were good in law; but English law had never yet been known to guard a woman's rights. No English queen had ever reigned alone, and in her native strength. Elizabeth was herself the lawful queen; but she was only reigning as her husband's wife. Nor could she hope her children would succeed where she, and others of their race, had

failed. She longed to see more heirs about her knee; male heirs; accepted heirs; indisputable heirs. The King was still more restive than herself; his regal pride, his turn for peace, his hope of founding one great monarchy on English soil, conspired to rouse in him that passion for male offspring which is seldom dead in any human soul. In him, this passion glowed and raged. Prince Arthur's liking for his winsome bride gave both his parents promise that their court might soon be gladdened by the light of future kings.

3. A pale and oval face, a pair of dreamy eyes, a delicate lip and mouth, gave Arthur an air and grace not found in his robust and sturdy brother. Henry was at ten as big as Arthur at fifteen. Though lithe and comely, Arthur caused men's eyes to turn from him in fear. He was a prince of Camelot, a prince of song and legend; and they turned with hope from Dr. Bereworth's patient, to the ruddy cheek and stalwart frame of Henry, Duke of York.

4. Elate with joy, and tasting of a freedom she had never known in Spain, the Princess rode to Chertsey Abbey on the Thames; the abbey built by Erkenwald, the famous Saxon saint, who was to be so much with Catharine in her bridal days. At Chertsey she was lodged and feasted; and the next day came towards Kingston, where a goodly company of lords and ladies—Edward Duke of Buckingham, George Earl of Kent, Edward Lord Dudley, William Lord Stourton, the Abbot of Bury, and a band of gentlemen and pages, gave her a merry "welcome to the realm." With lengthening

train she rode—the Lord High Constable in front, the squires and yeomanry behind her, to St. George's Fields, near Lambeth, where a still more goodly company stood ready to receive her. There she first saw Henry, Duke of York. Near Henry stood that Thomas Savage who had signed the treaty of Medina del Campo, and in compliment to her had just been raised to the Archbishopric of York. Near him, again, were Richard Fox, Lord Privy Seal and Bishop of Winchester; Henry, Earl of Essex; Father Thomas, Abbot of St. Albans; and Father John, Abbot of Westminster; with upwards of a hundred barons, knights, and gentlemen of rank. Each baron was attended by his squire and page, adorned with feather, sword, and cloak. So brave a show had not been seen for many a year; and not the least worth seeing was that boy of ten who sat his charger like a king, and parleyed with the bride, though her dueña scowled in his unflinching face. The Princess was beside herself with joy.

5. Yet near her mule, and near the Duke of York, stood two great courtiers, cap in hand, whose blood was by and bye to mingle in the veins of one who was to be her rival in the palace, her successor on the throne. These two great courtiers were Thomas Howard, Earl of Surrey, and Sir William Boleyn, one of a hundred knights who rode in company of the Duke of York.

6. Thomas, Earl of Surrey, was a son of that John Howard, first Duke of Norfolk of the Howard line, who fell on Bosworth Field. A young and splendid captain, brave as Bayard, prudent as Gon-

salvo, he had opened his career beneath the happiest stars. Having learnt the art of war from Charles the Bold, he had returned to England, where his father was devoted to the House of York, and served with high repute at Lincoln, Banbury, and Barnet. He had won the woman of his heart, Elizabeth Tilney, widow of his cousin, Sir Humphrey Bourchier, and had seen his house at Ashewolthorpe grow merry with a numerous offspring. Honours had been showered upon him. He was created Earl of Surrey; he was elected Knight of the Garter; he was made the Sheriff of two counties. On the field of Bosworth he had led the archers, and, except the King, had been the greatest hero on the losing side. But Fortune had betrayed her favourite. His honours lost, his lands escheated, and his liberty restrained, Surrey had moped for many months a prisoner in the Tower. A striking word had set the hero free. When Simnel was at Newark, on his way to London, the Lieutenant of the Tower had gone into his cell, and offered him the keys. "My lord, you are at liberty to go, if you so please." But Surrey would not take the keys. "The King has sent me hither; and I will not stir till he command me hence." The false Lieutenant must have been surprised. "On your allegiance, sir," the Earl had said, "I charge you, if the King is yet alive, to bring me to him, that I may assist his Grace." A knight, susceptible to knightly feeling, Henry had embraced his prisoner, set him free, restored his blood, and given him back the property of his wife. Thomas, his eldest son, was decorated with the George and Garter. Edward, his second son, was knighted in the field. Elizabeth, his wife, was mistress of the Princess's household. As the crown of all his heir was married to the peerless Lady Anne Plantagenet, sister of the Queen. This lovely woman had been pledged to Philip the Fair; she had been courted by Manoel of Portugal; she had been asked in marriage by the Prince of Scotland; but the heir of Surrey had secured her. No one doubted that this highly favoured soldier would regain the ducal coronet which his father, John, had lost, and which his wife, Elizabeth, was allowed by royal grace to wear. High service was atoning for his first and last offence. He signed the treaty of Etaples with the King of France; he fought against the northern rebels and the titular Duke of York; he was assisting in the match of Princess Margaret with the King of Scots. Great offices were showered upon him and his family. He was General of the Forces, Admiral in the Narrow Seas, Sub-warden of the Marches, and Lord High Treasurer of England.

7. Sir William Boleyn was a son of Godfrey Boleyn, of the Jewry, mercer, alderman, and mayor. Godfrey was a son of Geoffrey Boleyn, also of the Jewry; in the little church of which locality these worthies sleep. A family of French descent, who came to London for the sake of trade, the Boleyns chose to stay in England after they had filled their chests and ceased to toil in mart and shop. Yet they had never dropped their French connexion. As they grew in riches, adding house to house, and park to park, they had been lifting up their eyes in

wedlock, and improving lowly blood by that of nobly-born and handsome wives. Sir Godfrey, mayor and city knight, had married Anne, the only child of Thomas, Baron Hoo and Hastings; and Sir William, eldest son of Godfrey by this heiress of the Hoos, had married Lady Margaret, second daughter and co-heiress of the Earl of Carrick and Ormonde. Anne and Lady Margaret had brought into the Boleyn family a claim, not only on the baronies of Hoo and Hastings, but on the earldoms of Carrick and Ormonde, and in more remote degree on the earldom of Wiltshire. Married to the daughter of a man who held two earldoms, and had some pretensions to a third, Sir William had retired from business in the Jewry and become a gentleman at court. The lord of Blickling Hall and Hever Castle; one a great estate in Norfolk, and the second a delicious seat in Kent; could make a figure with the best; and nothing but the best would satisfy this offspring of the city knight. He matched his eldest son, Sir Thomas, with Lady Elizabeth Howard, Surrey's eldest daughter, and he gave them Hever Castle as a home. This marriage brought Sir William what he wanted: a connexion with the highest orders in the kingdom. Lady Elizabeth was the daughter of a duchess, and her brother was married to a sister of the Queen. Sir William Boleyn therefore was a close connexion of the royal family; and his son, Sir Thomas, and that son's wife, Lady Elizabeth, a woman of entrancing beauty, were persons in attendance on the King and Queen.

8. Not dreaming of the webs which Fate was

weaving for them down in Kent, the Duke of York and Catharine rode together from St. George's Fields to Lambeth House. The Cardinal who had made himself the patron of her love-affairs, was gone to his account; and Father Henry Deane, Augustine monk and Deputy in Ireland, had succeeded Morton as Archbishop of Canterbury. Deane had also taken upon himself a special patronage of the match. Beneath his roof at Lambeth, Catharine was to rest until her entry into London and her marriage to the Prince of Wales.

CHAPTER X.

Bridals.

1501.

1. PRINCE ARTHUR came to the Wardrobe, in Blackfriars, to be in readiness for his bridal day. He was not strong enough to bear fatigue, and Henry wished him to be near St. Paul's. The King and Queen dropped down the Thames from Sheen to Paris Gardens, then a pretty house belonging to the monks of Bermondsey, from which the Queen went on to Lambeth House; while Henry, who had not seen the Princess since his interview at Dogmersfield, pushed over in his barge to Baynard's Castle, near the river Fleet. He had rebuilt this ancient castle, not as in the Norman days, with keep and moat, with tower and wall, but in the new domestic style; rebuilt it as a house and home, in which the Queen could hold her court without being fretted by the sight of mounted guns and men equipped for war. This house, a type of his new England, he proposed to give the Prince and Princess for their future home.

2. The Queen was pleased with the Infanta, whom she found in company of her maids, dueñas, and confessors. If the Spanish girl was not of ravishing beauty, like her sister the Archduchess,

yet, compared against such girls as Beatrix and Inez, she was bright and fair. Her women wore a dress of black and white, and had their veils drawn close about the face. Elizabeth thought her son was happy in his choice. The King was free of hand; not sparing either pains or money to adorn her future home; and sending into foreign parts for plate "against the marriage of my lord the prince." He hired good houses in the city for his Spanish guests, and gave to each a proof of his esteem:— to the Archbishop of Santiago, five hundred marks; to the Bishop of Majorca, four hundred marks; to Count de Cabra, three hundred marks; and to the rest according to their rank.

3. The nuptial day was fixed for Sunday, November the fourteenth, a local festival of St. Erkenwald, the Saxon saint. This local festival was kept in Cheape and Lombard Street as well as in the cloister and the church; St. Erkenwald being to London citizens what St. Thomas was to those of Canterbury. A Saxon prince, the saint had spent his time in reading holy books and building cells for monks and nuns, until King Sebba had compelled him to accept a pastoral staff. As bishop of London he had laboured in his office many years; had much enlarged St. Paul's; had gained high privileges for the altar; and had left the citizens his sacred dust. So potent was this dust that almost every one was cured who knelt before his shrine. A chip of wood from his horse-litter had cured diseases after he was dead. St. Erkenwald was the popular London saint. His day was given to prayer

and sport. His ashes were the consecration of St. Paul's, where crowds of penitents and pilgrims thronged his shrine, and drew from him a sacred and refining fire.

4. What priest and monk could do to bring a blessing on the nuptial day was done. The saints were all invoked. A figure of St. Catharine was arrayed in costly robes, and taught to compliment the royal maid. The cells and cloisters rang with praise of Spain. From distant convents monks marched up to London, and increased the general stir and joy. All bishops were enjoined to throw their houses open and to spread their boards with meat and drink. But few required this hint from Deane. The Church regarded Catharine as her child, and Catharine's union with the Prince as her peculiar work. Nor were the temporal peers behind the spiritual peers. Along the river bank the houses were ablaze with flags and streamers. Every one put on his badge and cognizance. All servants were enjoined to don their masters' liveries, and the royal servants were so numerous that the streets seemed streaked with Tudor green and white. A gallant wore his lady's colours, and his form of greeting was a compliment to the sex. Nor were the citizens behind the peers in festive and pictorial pomp. They wore their brightest robes, and dressed their shops with flags and poles. A vat of ale was broached in every street. A table stood at almost every door. So great a holiday had not been known in London since the civil wars had broken out.

5. On Friday morning, Henry, Duke of York,

arrived at Catharine's door, attended by a gallant band, to lead her through the City, where she had not yet been seen, and lodge her at the Bishop's palace in the shadow of St. Paul's. This palace was untenanted; for Savage, who had lived there, was removed to York; and William Warham, his successor in the see of London, was not yet installed. The traditional palace of the Saxon prince, St. Erkenwald, was placed at Catharine's service by the church. The Duke of York, already taller than herself, though he was six years younger, set her on a mule with gorgeous housings, and conveyed her through the gateways of the bridge, up Fish Street Hill, by Gracechurch Street, and so through Cornhill, past the Stock market, into Cheape, through thronging crowds, and under arches, flags, and poles. The Duke was on her right, the papal legate on her left; and thus it chanced, as men recalled the fact in after years, that when the young Infanta entered London, she was seen by every one between her future husband and the minister of Rome. All London flocked to see the Princess enter, and to bid her welcome as an English girl come home. Near London Bridge a group of mummers played for her the story of St. Catharine. Near the Standard in Cornhill, three houses had been taken for the King, the Queen, and Prince of Wales. A group of yeomen of the guard in Tudor colours filled the street below. In Cheape the Mayor and Sheriffs stayed her march by an address, a pageant, and a psalm. At every porch a priest came out with acolyte and choir; from every steeple rang a peal of bells;

from every window hung a flag; from every conduit ran a stream of wine. Each street through which she rode that day was filled with noise and colour; here a City guild with horn and tabard; there a monkish brotherhood with chant and crucifix; and here again, a troop of men-at-arms, a band of watermen, a company of apprentice boys, with all the lasses of their love, as frisky and as noisy as the men.

6. The royal maid was like a star. Arrayed in gold and silk, she wore a great round hat, from under which her bright red tresses floated in the wind. Elvira wore a nun-like dress, a habit black as night, with hanging sleeve of serge, and band of linen round her brow. The maids of honour, Inez, Beatrix, Maria, and Francisca, sat on mules; for none of these poor riders could be got to mount an English jennet. Everything was done to gratify her pride and stimulate her love. A lady held the rein for each of her four maids of honour. The Archbishop of Santiago rode abreast with the Archbishop of York, the Bishop of Majorca with the Bishop of Winchester, the Count de' Cabra with the Duke of Buckingham, and so on through her long and splendid train. But no one in that gay procession through the City took the public eye so much, nor dwelt upon the mind so long, as that stout boy and that fair woman riding side by side; a papal legate on their flank, an abbess-like dueña in their rear; the gallant boy and rosy woman answering to the cheers with stately courtesies and beaming smiles. Before she passed into her chamber for the night, she knelt and prayed before St. Erkenwald's shrine.

7. On Sunday, November 14, St. Erkenwald's local festival, the Duke of York again came for her to the Bishop's house. He came as soon as it was day; for Catharine was to be a wife by ten o'clock. When all was ready for the march, he led her from her chamber to the church, attended by Elizabeth Duchess of Norfolk, mistress of her household, by Elvira her dueña, by the maids of honour, and a flutter of the foremost peers and ladies in the kingdom. As she stept into the street all eyes were fixed on her attire; a veil of silk and pearls which hid her face; a gown of ample width, stuck out below the waist with hoops. A blare of trumpets greeted her, while cannon fired, and bells flung out their music on the air. He led her up the nave into the transept, where a stage had been erected, and where Arthur and his knights and pages were in waiting for the bride. As well became a prince of Camelot, her bridegroom, Arthur, was arrayed from cap to shoe in spotless white. All those who had become her friends by helping to promote the match were present in the church. Her patron, Deane, was ready to perform the rite. Fox, Bishop of Winchester, King, Bishop of Bath and Wells, and Smyth, Bishop of Lincoln, were arrayed in full pontificals in honour of the day. A crowd of bishops, mitred abbots, deans and priors, stood near the platform. Nave and aisle were filled. The King and Queen looked down on the imposing scene. When Catharine reached the platform, Deane began the service, that in fusing two young lives in one was meant to bind two great and powerful nations to pursue a common

course. The Count de Cabra gave away the bride; the Archbishop of Santiago and the Bishop of Majorca joined in the recitals and responses. Stepping from the platform, Arthur and his bride advanced in full procession with the prelates, followed by a band of singers and a press of peers and knights, to the great altar-steps, where all the company knelt down before St. Erkenwald's tomb. Then mass was said and canticle was sung by the attendant priests and choir. No match of English prince had ever seemed more pleasing to the popular heart; no marriage rite had ever been conducted with a higher pomp. When Deane pronounced a blessing on the bride and groom, the great Cathedral seemed to sigh with the response—Amen!

BOOK THE SEVENTH.
ARTHUR AND CATHARINE.

CHAPTER I.

Honeymoon.

1501.

1. HENRY OF GREENWICH, standing near the bride, received her at the altar from the primate, and conducted her through press of peers and dames, while Arthur of Winchester stayed behind in spectral white among the crowd of lawyers, priests, and monks. Along the Gothic nave they passed; through lines of peers and ladies, in array of purple, green, and gold; of aldermen in crimson gowns, and abbots in their high pontificals; all eyes upon them, from those of King and Queen to Rede, the new Lord Mayor, and the companions of his state. Loud blasts of trumpets hailed them on the steps. A train of guns flashed out; a hundred bells gave tongue; and throats from every door and window roared a welcome to the bride. A guard, in Tudor green and white, had kept a lane for them, and in the midst of colour, light, and music, they descended from the church,

and, followed by a band of archers carrying halberds, passed into the Bishop's house.

2. Arthur stayed behind with priests and lawyers to complete the act of settlement. Before the altar, and the ashes of St. Erkenwald, with peers and knights for witnesses, he settled on his bride a third part of his goods and rents. His act was then proclaimed by heralds from the western door, on which the citizens rent the welkin with their shouts. Prince Arthur's marriage was an act of peace, and no event since Henry was united to Elizabeth of York had pleased the English folk so highly as the match with Spain. The Prince was moved by their applause, and noticing the new Lord Mayor among the crowd, he sent his steward of the household, Richard Croft, to ask him and his brethren of the crimson gown to dine.

3. Attended by his knights and squires, Charles Brandon, Robert Ratcliffe, Antony Willoughby, and Maurice St. John, Arthur passed to his apartments in the palace, where a table had been spread. The King, who treated government as a splendid art, had taken care that everything was done to make the full amount of show. A Spaniard knew the price of gold and silver ware, and that on Arthur's table, where the bride and groom sat down to feast, was worth not less than twenty thousand pounds. Ayala marked each cup and dish—the shape, the chasing, and the mass—and Santiago was surprised to see such signs of wealth and taste in the far-northern isle. A full description of that plate was sent to Spain. With song and supper, night came down;

for night comes early on November afternoons; and then the Duchess of Norfolk, Doña Elvira, and the maids of honour came in state, and took the bride away, while Arthur and his gentlemen retired into the Prince's private room. A priest was brought into the nuptial chamber, and the usual prayer being said, the youthful bride and groom were blessed according to the forms laid down by holy Church.

4. Their honeymoon was spent in state, and no one in their household had a doubt that boy and girl were truly man and wife. In street and church, at joust and ring, they were observed together, happy in each other's eyes. Among the closer witnesses of their married love were Duchess Elizabeth, Agnes Tilney, Robert Ratcliffe, Antony Willoughby, and Padre Alessandro. Bereworth kept an eye on Arthur; for the youth was not robust: and such a change of life as that from rural Eltham, where he had been living with his sister Margaret and his blind old tutor André, to excited London, with the round of masques and plays, of jousts and revels, was enough to try a stouter frame than his. From house to house, from dance to dance, the Prince of Camelot bore his youthful bride. Due show was made for them in Westminster, where the King and Queen were present, with the Lady Margaret and the Duke of York. A joust was held in presence of a mighty throng; a pageant and a banquet followed in the hall; which Henry had contrived to hang with tapestry and cloth of gold, pricked out by flags and spears. He wished to make the Count de Cabra and Don Pedro de Ayala own that even

in Toledo and Medina they had never seen a braver sight. The banners and devices were Arthurian, and the legends were connected with Sir Lancelot, Guinevere, and the blameless king. Courtney, the Queen's brother-in-law, rode a red dragon, led by a giant. Edward, Duke of Buckingham, appeared in armour, as a knight of Arthur's court, and challenged every one to try a lance in honour of these royal nuptials. Thomas, Marquis of Dorset, half-brother of the Queen, took up his challenge. Each was followed into the arena by a train of knights and squires, and when the rival peers had snapt their shafts, the knights and yeomen closed in fight. So brave a joust had not been seen for many a day; and Catharine was unable to decide between her knights. As Queen of Beauty, she bestowed a ring on each; conferring them as prizes they had fairly won.

5. The company retired into the palace, where a feast was followed by a ball. While Arthur, Prince of Wales, looked on, his brother Henry led his sister out to dance. A child of striking beauty, as her portraits witness, Lady Margaret divided the attention of that sparkling company with the new Princess of Wales. Though hardly twelve years old, she, too, was going to be a bride. An embassy had come from Stirling with a formal offer on the part of James, the King of Scots; an embassy consisting of Robert Blacater, Archbishop of Glasgow, Patrick, Earl of Bothwell, Andrew Forman, Postulate of Moray, and the eminent poet, William Dunbar. These Scottish gentlemen were seated in a place of

honour near the King. As Henry led his sister out, a thousand eyes were bent on her—a hope of union and a pledge of peace between the two great branches of the English race. The boy and girl began to leap and reel, until the Prince, who found his robes too stiff for dancing, flung them off, and finished the performance in his jacket, to the great delight of every one who saw them, and especially of the King and Queen.

6. These days of Catharine's honeymoon were passed in scenes arranged by Henry to engage her mind and charm her eye. The Prince seemed fond of her, as lover should be of his bride. From Richmond palace, whither they retired from Baynard Castle, Arthur wrote to tell the King and Queen of Spain that he had never felt such joy as when he saw her blooming face. No woman in the world, he said, could be to him what Catharine was; and he declared that he would be to her a true and loving husband all his days. No one supposed that they were not canonically man and wife. Cabra and Ayala could not be deceived. They had Fernando's orders not to pay the first instalment of her dowry till they learned that she was married to the Prince according to the full and perfect law of Rome. They sought for proofs; they satisfied their minds; they took the money down to Richmond; and in presence of Johannes Cañazares, apostolic notary, they paid to Henry's officers a hundred thousand crowns.

7. Their honeymoon was hardly spent in this gay round of pleasure, ere the Prince's fading cheek alarmed the Queen. Advice was taken on the point;

advice of councillors, as well as of physicians; for the matter had a public side no less important than the personal side. Fernando wished the boy and girl to live beneath a common roof and always in each other's sight. He longed for heirs. As yet his dynasty was insecure. Of all his children, only one, Juana, had a son; Don Carlos, born in Ghent, and heir to an imperial throne. He yearned to hear that Arthur was the father of a Prince of Wales. The English court was no less eager than the Spanish King, and Henry was induced to close his ear on those who spoke to him of Arthur's paling cheek. He merely parted them a week or so, by sending Arthur to a country house while Catharine kept her lodging near the King and Queen.

CHAPTER II.

Catharine's Plate.

1501.

1. THE bride and groom had not been many days apart, when Henry raised the question of their going down to Ludlow Castle, where he meant his son to keep a model court, and live again the legends of his race. Old servants shook their heads. The case of Juan and Marguerite was recalled, but Henry was so much excited by his letters out of Spain, that he forgot the interests of his crown. In Spain, they would not hear of Catharine leaving Arthur for a day; and out of deference to the Spanish court the King consented that the bride and groom should go to Wales. A council and a household were selected with the utmost care. A bishop, William Smyth, of Lincoln, was appointed President of the Council, and Sir Richard Pole, a near connexion of the Queen, was made the chamberlain of their household. Smyth and Pole were aged men and trusty councillors. Smyth was one of "the caitiffs and villains of simple birth" denounced in Warbeck's proclamation. Pole was a man of family, who had married Margaret Plantagenet, a daughter of George, Duke of Clarence, and a cousin of the reigning Queen. Bereworth was to travel with his

patient. Ludlow, as the later Camelot, was to see a fearless hero and a loving wife within her walls. Prince Arthur and the Princess Catharine were to hold a perfect court; and prove to all the world how easily poetic legends could be melted into actual life.

2. Some baser thought was mixed with this poetic gold; some thought of how the King might gain the use, and afterwards obtain possession, of the Spanish plate. By treaty, Catharine's plate and jewels, both the vessels of her table and the ornaments of her person, were to count as portions of her dowry; to be valued and received as so much money when the last instalment should be due. A hundred thousand scudos had been paid; within a year a fresh instalment of fifty thousand scudos would be due; and in another year a third instalment must be paid. This third instalment would consist of fifty thousand scudos paid in gold, fifteen thousand scudos paid in silver plate, and twenty thousand scudos paid in diamonds and other precious stones. Demand for other terms had failed. He wished the King and Queen of Spain to give their daughter dish and chalice, ring and necklace, as became her rank, not counting them as dowry; but the King and Queen insisted that these trinkets must be reckoned as a part of her two hundred thousand crowns. He was not pleased with the affair; the King and Queen of Spain, he thought, were acting meanly towards their child; and he was tempted to repay them in their own base coin. Unhappily, a Spanish agent was at hand to guess his

wishes and to show him how to cheat the King and Queen.

3. Since Puebla came to London, though his purse was fuller than of yore, he had not changed the manner of his life. He still consorted with the low and vile. He housed with dollies and apprentice lads, and used his rank as an ambassador to screen the dens in which he lodged. Strange stories having reached his master's ears, the King of Spain had sent two spies to London for the purpose of observing and reporting what they found. These spies, Fray Johannes de Matienzo, sub-prior of Santa Cruz, and Sancho de Londoño, knight commander, had not been many weeks in London ere they drew a comic picture of the man who represented Kaiser, King, and Pope in Henry's court. According to the spies, the stories told of him in Spain were true. Puebla had taken a lodging in a mason's house; a house of evil name; in which the master made his gains by lodging common drabs and robbing fools who frequented his den. Dining at a common table with this dubious company, he paid no more than twopence for his fare. He had his freedom of the house, for which he gave his name to any of the city watch who came to search the house in quest of stolen goods. He lent small sums of money to the poor, and seized their substance to repay his loans. From nearly every foreigner who lived in London he contrived to wring a fee. He sold his offices in the court and city, and his nearness with the King enabled him to deal in pardons, licenses, and grants. As Spanish envoy, he had jurisdiction

over every Spaniard in the realm; and when a Spaniard came to him for justice, he expected and received a bribe. All this Fernando heard, and yet he had maintained the cripple in his place. Like Henry, he had need for men of various talents; and a priest who cost him nothing, and would act on half a hint, in causes which no honest man would touch, was not an agent whom he could replace.

4. If Henry used a tone of mockery in speaking of this priest, he had no wish to see a better man sent out. He could not always satisfy the cripple's greed; and he had set his face against promoting him to the episcopal bench. Not once, but many times, the Spanish doctor had requested Henry to reward his faithful service with preferment in the Church, though he was well aware that men with physical defects were not invested with the pastoral staff. The King had jested with him; saying he must reward so good a priest, and asking which he would prefer, a benefice or a wife? Puebla had been coy. "Why not a bishopric?" Henry had rejoined: "for who would grace a mitre with a finer portliness of frame?" Too obviously the King was laughing, and the cripple had refused to look that way for payment. Then a wife had been proposed; a rich and buxom widow, who might be a comfort to him in his lonely state; but Puebla had been married once before, and having children living, had no mind to take a second wife. He had another and a better plan. A procurator in the Roman court had given him a thousand crowns to get a letter from the King of Spain to Alexander the Sixth,

recommending that official for a Cardinal's hat. Puebla had not been able to procure that letter from his master, and the procurator was requesting him to pay that money back. Would Henry give his vacant mitre to that procurator, and in that way cancel Puebla's obligation for the thousand crowns?

5. "Your Grace shall see," said Puebla to the King, "how much I take pains for you, in what I have obtained from my sovereign lords." He held a letter in his hand in Spanish. "By this letter you will learn that the thirty-five thousand ducats which you are to receive in jewels, pearls, gold, silver, and tapestry, in the last instalment of the dowry, will be given to you at once." The King was taken by surprise. If Puebla spoke the truth, he was to get a portion of the dowry long before the sum was due. The gain to him was clear, and when the bridal feasts were done, he sent for Juan de Cuero, keeper of the Spanish plate, and bade him hand it over to an English keeper. Cuero said there must be some mistake. His orders from his master were precise. He was to have the plate and jewels weighed and priced; to get receipts from Henry for their value; but he was to keep them in his hand, and hold them under lock and key, until the third instalment should be due. Enraged at this rebuff, the King called Puebla to his cabinet. Was he, or was he not, to have possession of the plate? Must he be told to give receipts for vessels which remained in Cuero's hands? Puebla affected to be sorely grieved. In zeal for Henry's service he had read his letter wrongly. Yes; the plate must lie in

Cuero's keeping; but he whispered in the royal ear, that this arrangement might be better for the King than any other they could make. The plan of which they had been speaking might have given the King possession some few months earlier than the stipulated date, but the plan he had to offer now would give him Catharine's jewels, not as part and payment of her dowry, but as something like a present from the King of Spain.

6. Suspecting that the priest was trying, for a purpose of his own, to draw him into taking up a false position, Henry waited. "If your Grace will keep my secret," Puebla whispered, "I will tell you how it is that I, your servant, have arranged this matter so; and if your Highness will accept my services, I promise to conduct affairs in such a fashion that the Princess shall keep her jewels, plate, and tapestry, and my sovereign lords shall pay their price to you as well." A ruler worn in worldly ways could hardly hear such words without a start. "The plan is this," said Puebla, shortly. "Let the Princess wear these jewels on her person, let her use these cups and covers on her table. She will learn to treat them as her own. The time for payment comes; you will refuse to take them as her dowry—as you have a right to do. My sovereign lords will not, for very shame, be able to remove the dishes from her table and the jewels from her neck. Your Grace will get the money and the plate." As Henry looked incredulous, Puebla whispered, "I have spoken with the Princess; she will act with us; the business can be done as I have said."

CHAPTER III.

To Ludlow.

1501.

1. Acting on Puebla's hint, the King pursued a course which Puebla would have envied, as a masterstroke. First, he went to Catharine's chamber, to remove, by smiles and phrases, the effect produced upon her mind by his demand on Cuero for her plate. Finding Elvira and Ayala in her room, he caught them to his sleeve, and spoke to the dueña and the proto-notary of all that he had said and done. Aware how much Elvira and Ayala hated Puebla, he delighted them by saying that the envoy was to blame for everything that was going wrong. He was to blame, and no one else. Turning to the Princess, he went on: "My lady daughter, although it might be well for you and me, if it were done as Puebla said it would be, and your parents gave you these things without counting them, yet I am not inclined to seek for an advantage. I am sorry to have asked your servant for the plate. I see there was a crafty scheme, but no one shall allege that it was mine. I am content to stand upon the treaty, and I beg you will inform the King and Queen that it was Puebla's error,—perhaps a wilful error, meant to trick us all. No thought of asking

for your plate had ever come into my mind till Puebla spoke to me. He must have had some wicked purpose in his heart; it was an artful trick; and he has doubtless told some other lie in Spain. It seems to me a heavy breach of trust. I beg of you, my lady daughter, and of you, Elvira, and of you, Don Pedro, to inform their highnesses of the truth. I would not have them think of me as one who asks for what is not his due. God be praised, I am not in want. If need were to arise, I might, for love of them, and of my daughter, spend a million of gold and not go into debt." Assured that things would be reported well, he left them; and began to shape his means for carrying Puebla's plans into effect.

2. An easy way was to allow the Prince and Princess to keep house together; using Catharine's cups and dishes for the common table; but in such a way that this result should seem to spring from accident, and not from choice. He thought this easy plan would suit him. Every one had heard that Arthur was to live in Ludlow. Every one at court was busy with the details of his journey and his settlement. It was a great affair, and needed time to perfect. Smyth, his president, was helping to select the members of his council. Pole, his chamberlain, was helping to select the officers of his household. Both were men of such repute and station that a crowd of knights and gentlemen were anxious to take service under them. Smyth was Chancellor of Oxford University as well as Bishop of Lincoln. Pole, a Knight of the Garter, was the husband of Lady Margaret, the Queen's first cousin

of the royal blood. No little had been done, and few could tell how much remained to do before the Prince could take his leave.

3. If groom and bride were sent away in haste, in seeming deference to Fernando's wish, it might be said that Arthur's household were not yet prepared, and Pole would need the use of Catharine's plate. The first step was for Pole to get her silver into daily use. Ayala was invited to the royal closet, where the King requested his advice. By usage of his realm, he said, the Prince should pass some months of every year in Wales. The details of his journey were arranged; but in the privy council there were two opinions as to whether he should go alone. The matter was so grave, that he could hardly see his way; for while his prudence as a father would have led him to agree with those who argued that the Prince should go alone, his love for Catharine and his deference to the wishes of her parents drew him to the side of those who would not part the groom and bride. What was Ayala's view? Ayala was not caught. Of all the men who came near Henry, he could see most clearly through the royal mind. He knew what Henry wished—that he, the Spanish agent, should insist on Catharine going to Ludlow; so that Pole might say there was no time to form a separate household, and the Spanish plate would have to be employed. Ayala answered dryly that he thought it might be wiser for the Prince to go alone.

4. Unable to entrap the proto-notary, the King went back to Catharine, whom he told of Arthur's

journey into Wales, the court and state he meant to keep at Ludlow, the advice of some that he should go alone, the doubts which troubled him as king and father, and his wish to please her in the whole affair. What was her will? He meant to leave her free. If she desired to go, she should. He loved her, and he would not interfere. He had no will but hers, whatever councillors and doctors might suggest. Of course, he had his fears, but in a case so near to her, she must decide what she would do. He only sought to know her mind. Would she prefer to go? She answered that *his* will was hers; that she had no ambition save to please him; that he must decide for her, not she for him; that what he fixed must surely be the best. So meek an answer was but little to his taste. He wanted Catharine to be high and proud. He begged her not to leave this choice to him; for though he loved her well, and hoped to please her always, he might miss her secret mind, and cause her to regret that she had put her trust in him. But Catharine would not say a second word. Annoyed at this repulse, he set his son, the Prince, to work on her. Then Arthur begged his wife to see the King, his father, and procure his leave for her to go; but Catharine, acting on Ayala's orders, told her husband she must leave this matter with the King. Four days were spent in these intrigues, and then Ayala heard, through agents in the court, that orders were being given for Catharine's journey into Wales, and that the Prince and she might leave at any hour. He heard, too, that the King was counting on the plate and jewels being carried down by Catharine for her ordinary use. Again, he spoke to Henry on the subject, calling in Elvira to confirm his speech. Elvira backed him, not as tendering an opinion of her own, but as a servant of her sovereigns, who had given her orders what to say. Ayala and Elvira told the King their sovereigns would prefer that Catharine should remain at court, and that the Prince, her husband, should reside in Wales alone. The King professed to be amazed; they must have read their letters badly; for his chief inducement to admit her going to the country was a strong entreaty of the King and Queen of Spain, conveyed to him by their most trusty agents, not to part their daughter from his son. These men of trust had told him that if Arthur went to Wales alone, the King and Queen would be incensed, and Catharine in despair.

5. Who could have told his Highness such a tale? At first, the King refused to say. Ayala grew more eager. On the point being pressed, he answered that he got his information from the Spanish chaplain and the Spanish envoy. Taken by surprise, Ayala held his tongue. Too well he knew his royal patrons not to fear that they were working out their schemes by double agencies and crooked paths. If Alessandro had been told to speak, as Henry hinted, he was likely to have spoken for the Queen. He was her officer. He had served her long, and knew the secrets of her heart. If Alessandro had been urging him to send the Princess into Wales, he must have done so by the Queen's

express command. To save the Spanish plate, Ayala had been venturing somewhat near the brink. If Henry were to take him at his word, and let the Prince depart without his wife, the Queen, her mother, might reprove his zeal. The ground beneath his feet was loose. What could he do, save write for fresh commands? In long and secret cyphers to the Queen, he poured out all his fears. He told her Highness everything. He more than hinted that Doctor Puebla was a scamp, and more than hoped that Padre Alessandro might be called to Spain. This honest priest was not a man for courts.

6. Until Ayala got fresh orders out of Spain, his hands were bound, and Henry could dispose of Catharine and her flagons as he pleased. He settled she should go to Wales. Before she left, the priests and soldiers who had come with her from Spain were called to court and thanked with royal words and gifts. Cups, rings, books, pictures, were bestowed on every one. At last, they took their leave, and having done their duty, rode away; Fonseca going straight to Spain by sea, while Cabra went by way of Calais to the Archduke's court. When they were gone, the Princess sank; but Henry knew the way to soothe such girlish griefs. He took her to his cabinet, where he showed her, first, his books and prints, all rich with rare conceits and humours, and, at last, a tray of rings and bracelets. She was told to choose her own, and when her choice was made, the rest were given as compliments to her maids.

7. On Tuesday morning, December 21st, the

Prince and Princess rode away from London. Every day they held a feast, and every night they slept beneath a sacred or a noble roof. A change was made among the officers of Catharine's household, which was gall and wormwood to the principal lady of her suite. Manrique, her first chamberlain, quarrelled with Cuero, second chamberlain and keeper of the plate. Pedro Manrique was Elvira's husband; Elvira was of noble birth; and Pedro could not brook the insolence of a second chamberlain. Both officers were in the wrong; and Pole, who had a grudge against Manrique, seized the moment of their quarrel to degrade them both. Elvira could not save her husband from the ire of Pole. Instead of chamberlain, Manrique was degraded to the rank of usher. From the post of second chamberlain, Cuero was reduced to that of second usher. Pole, now chamberlain of both the households, took upon himself the management of every one about the royal pair. He had no further trouble with the Spanish plate. A merry Christmas met them on the road; and through the Christmas days they rode on happily towards their castle in the border land. One trouble only seemed to lie on Arthur's mind. His sister, Lady Margaret, the playmate of his youth at Eltham, was in London, in the midst of ministers and prelates who were wrangling with each other on the policy of sending her to Stirling as a Queen of Scots.

CHAPTER IV.

The Scots.

1501-2.

1. THE coming of ambassadors from Stirling to arrange a match with Lady Margaret caused an eager curiosity in London as to what the Scots were like, and as to what the suitor, James, their King, was like? The truce was known to be unpopular beyond the Tweed; where hatred of the English court and people was at fever heat. The King of Scots was called a popular prince; yet in this business of an English marriage he was marching in the teeth of every passion in his realm. Would all these passions yield before his strength of will? What sort of men were they whom he would have to force? Few Londoners knew anything about the Scots, except as enemies; a rieving, thieving crew, who burst from year to year into the peaceful English shires, accompanied by savages more treacherous and ferocious than themselves; and who, when beaten back into their mountain lairs, spat forth their venom in satirical pasquils and lampoons. Their rhymes, in truth, had roused more enemies than their raids. A Saxon, who could answer blow with blow, was far less nimble in abusive phrases than a Scot. One biting word

had drawn an army to the north, and led to acts of vengeance on the Tweed. Instead of treating satire as the fence and play of men denied the use of nobler arms, an English courtier treated it as the venom spat by starving wolves. A citizen who had never seen his kinsmen of the north, was apt to think of them as no more human than a savage beast. These Scots, however, who had come to London seemed of other type. Robert, archbishop of Glasgow, was a man of dignified appearance. Bothwell was a gallant soldier. Forman was a scholar of the highest class. What sort of land and people had these gentlemen come to represent?

2. Ayala had described that country and that people for the King of Spain, and Trevisano had repeated part of his description for the Doge of Venice. With a few additions here and there, that picture of the Scots, when they appeared by deputies in Henry's court, will place them bodily before the reader's eye.

3. A wild and singular region was inhabited by these Scots. Their country was without a frontier and an outline. Lifted into mountain crests, and channelled by two stormy seas, with stretch of heathery moor and sweep of shining friths, she seemed to every one who had to climb her heights and cross her lakes, the picture of a lovely, scattered, and forlorn estate. From south to north, she lay extended on a line as long as that from Malaga to Roncesvalles, but not a little of her kingdom lay below the levels of her lochs and seas. Deep lakes

filled in her valleys. Friths ran up into her inland shires. Great passages of sea divided town from town. A group of isles and islets, tempting to the pirate, stretched from Cantire in the Irish waters to the almost arctic Unst. These isles were not all tenanted by man; but sixty-four of them were held in fee; and many of the isles had herds of sheep and swine. In time of war each isle lay open to attack; in time of peace each isle required some outlay for defence. Across the water dwelt a race of jarls and pirates, who, from ancient days, had scoured these northern waves in search of prey. If rye ran short in Bergen, or if seals were scarce in Tromsö, they had always put to sea and swept these islands bare. No force could stay their ravages. The islets lay too far apart for mutual help; and often, on account of local feuds, the settlers of one islet joined the strangers in their raid against the next. Nor was the mainland easier to defend and cultivate than the isles. Great ridges separated town from town; deep lakes and perilous friths divided shire from shire. A road was hard to make, and harder still to keep. The only open ways were water-ways. Bleak ridge, dark moor, and pathless glen shut up the country from itself, and yet, by a caprice of nature, almost every city in the land lay open to an enemy who came by sea.

4. Four races occupied this region; Saxon, Briton, Scot, and Pict; four races which had hardly anything in common, save their Catholic faith and hatred of the English name. The Saxons were the

ruling race. A Saxon wore the crown, and Saxons held the principal royal fiefs. The Saxons occupied the capital, the sea-ports, and the lowland shires. Beside these Saxons stood the Scots, an Irish tribelet, who had swept across the land, and stamped their name into the soil. The Scot was found in every shire; a hot and stalwart fellow; quick in love and ire; and ready to protect his own. Along the sea-coasts, from the Mull of Galloway, to the farthest isles, the Picts still lingered as a separate people, keeping up their ancient customs; and in every county there were remnants of the still more ancient Gaels. In English eyes, a Scot, a Briton, and a Pict were one; a beast of bony frame, of unkempt head, of filthy habit, and of greedy maw. All strangers in the country took this English view, and spoke of Briton, Scot, and Pict, as savages who lived in lonely glens and distant isles; who brayed and barked in uncouth dialects; mere mules and mastiffs to their Saxon lords. The fire and grace, the wit and valour, the fidelity and humour, the delight in ancient ways and reverence for an unseen power, which mark these races, each and all, were little in the masters' eye. Few Saxons learnt the Gaelic tongue, and fewer conned the treasuries of Gaelic verse. As yet, the English people had not come to see how well the fancy and the pathos of these ancient tribes would blend with the aggressive and enduring qualities of the younger race. The solvent of a common speech was still unsought; the solvent of a common rule was still unfound.

5. A stranger, living at the capital, would seldom

see these ancient and poetic clans, who lived away from towns, and made, as yet, no figure in the court. The fertile lowlands of the south were held by men of English stock, who spoke some dialect of English speech. In other days, these districts had been parcel of a Saxon kingdom. Saxon laws and usages prevailed in them; and Edinburgh, the capital, was as much an English town as York. When the old kingdom of Northumbria had been rent asunder, and a second border had been cut between the Solway and the Tweed, the men of this new border line had added to the bitterness of ordinary frontier feuds the passions of a people who are close of kin. A hundred times the border had been swept, and what was meant by border, in the larger meaning, is the country stretching from the gates of Stirling to the Yorkshire wolds. Sometimes the farms were stript of kine and sheep, and sometimes they were scorched of tree and shrub. From year to year, from reign to reign, this waste of life went on. No little of the lowlands had become a desert, which the hinds who lived by trapping game were glad to share with packs of wolves. A rage that knew no bounds had come to burn between these brethren of a former state. To live within the border was to live beyond the law. Not only farms and villages were spoiled, but convents were profaned and churches robbed. Although these lowlanders were men of English race, religion seemed to have no power upon them; for a gang of men-at-arms would ravage Melrose and Holyrood whom no persuasion could have moved to touch an English shrine.

6. The towns were few in number and were poor in population. All the towns save one were open; for the King could never trust his subjects with their own defence. Edinburgh had barely twenty thousand souls within her gates, yet she was far ahead of Glasgow, Aberdeen, and Perth. The elder capital, Perth, had about six thousand inhabitants. Glasgow and Aberdeen had under two thousand each. But if the towns were small, the houses in these towns were built of stone, and what was then uncommon, even in France and Italy, had proper doors and windows filled with glass. Each house had its own chimney; and a cunning eye, familiar with the mansions of Toledo, Rome, and Paris, found in Scottish houses an abundant share of arras, furniture, and plate. A close connexion with the court of France had introduced French luxuries into the house, French idioms into the language; but Ayala noticed in the Scottish houses that the better sort of furniture was old, and had been handed down from sire to son.

7. Three towns in Scotland were already Universities: St. Andrews, Aberdeen, and Glasgow; and the people of that country set a store on learning far beyond their neighbours in the South. More men of high repute were to be found in Scottish than in English towns. Dunbar was peerless. Few professors stood so high in science as Hay and Annand. Hector Boeis and Gawain Douglas left behind them memorable names. Nor was the fame

of Scottish science less renowned abroad. Alesse held the chair of theology in Leipzig, Dempster held the chair of philosophy in Paris, Scrimzeour held the chair of civil law in Geneva, Dickson held the chair of theology in Pavia. Many Scots, like Ferne and Gregory, were doctors of the Sorbonne. Sixty-three great abbeys,—such as Dryburgh, Kelso, and Holyrood,—with a yet greater number of inferior houses, testified the popular piety. Each abbey had a king for founder; and the lesser houses had their properties and rents. The clergy, as a learned class, enjoyed much power. Although the land was poor, she had two archbishops, eleven bishops, and more than sixty abbots, all of whom had good estates. In order to compete with these great prelates, men of secular rank, the Humes and Campbells, Kennedeys and Carrs, were forced to study hard, and gird themselves with arts as well as arms.

CHAPTER V.

King of Scots.

1501.

1. THE King of Scots was twenty-eight years old; a man of clear complexion; neither tall nor short, but of a noble height, and handsome as a king need be. His hair and beard were long, for he had neither clipt nor shorn them, and the fall of curling locks became him well. A master of the French and Latin tongues, he also spoke Italian, English, Dutch, and German. Nay, he understood Castillian, and was pleased when any one addressed him in that idiom. He knew the language of his savage subjects in the mountains and the isles. A Scottish prince had need to be a prodigy of speech. The ordinary Scottish idiom was as unlike English as Aragonese was unlike Castillian; and the language of his savage subjects differed from Scottish as Biscayan differed from Castillian. James knew everything. He had read his Bible much, and made a fair acquaintance with some other pious books. Histories were his pastime; histories in the French and Latin tongues; the best of which he had perused. He kept all precepts of his Church. Before he saw a man on business in the morning, he would hear two masses. Nothing would induce

him to eat flesh on Wednesday and Friday. He was fond of priest and monk, and, more than all, of an observant friar. St. Francis was his model of a working saint. To an observant friar he listened for advice; to an observant friar he made confession of his sins. The friars were in his chamber and his ante-room; about him when he slept and when he woke. To an observant friar he gave the abbot's mitre and the bishop's staff. Yet neither piety nor learning could be called his special note. Some other princes were as pious and as learned as the King of Scots. The special mark of James—distinction rarer in his day than love of letters and respect for holy things—was an imperious loyalty to his spoken word. A man of truth, he made a personal religion of adherence to his pledge. So scrupulous was he in his speech, that he would hardly make a joke, if it appeared to cover and conceal a lie. To the amusement of diplomatists grown hoary in deceit, he tried to do away with royal oaths. A king, he thought, should never swear. His word should be his bond. A king, in virtue of his royalty, was raised above the sphere of lies, and since he could not break his word, why should he bind himself by oath? To swear was to adopt a vow more binding than a spoken word, and to confess that fear of shame was not so strong as fear of hell.

2. His government was that of every feudal prince; a military lordship, tempered by the right of mutiny; a right which his lieutenants were not slow to use. The land was his; the folk were also

his; but fear restrained him from abusing his paternal trust. A king of Scots could do anything he liked, except prevent rebellion breaking out. The history of his house had been a tragedy. His father, James the Third, had been murdered as he lay in bed. His grandfather, James the Second, had been killed in border wars. His great-grandfather, James the First, had been assassinated in a Dominican convent. Upwards, into the remotest ages, it had always been the same. A king of Scots had been required to wear his crown and life upon his sword.

3. In physical courage, James was like a dog that flies at every object, even a shadow, in his path. When Surrey led an army to the north, he sent that English peer a challenge, offering to fight him, hand to hand, for Berwick. Surrey had no power to wager Berwick, and declined the combat, saying he was Henry's soldier, and was not at liberty to risk his life; but when the war was over, and his troops were gone to England, he would fight his Grace on either horse or foot. James was too hot of blood to be a prudent leader. At the clang of horns, he drew his sword, and dashed into the fight, forgetting that his duty was to watch and speak, and that the safety of his troops depended on the coolness of his head. Ayala followed him to the field, in order to restrain his headlong speed. At every blast he started to his feet. Ayala caught him by the skirts and held him back. "My subjects serve me in my quarrels, whether they are just or unjust," he observed, in answer to the

Spaniard; "so that, when they risk their lives, I ought to show myself in front." When war was done, he loved to hunt and shoot. No carpet chase was his, but rough and hungry mountain toil. By day he stalked the Highland deer; at night he slept in some poor herdsman's lodge. His power of abstinence surprised the Spanish priest. "I never saw a man so temperate out of Spain," Ayala wrote. He got up early, ate but little, drank still less, and worked at business hard and late. Quick, hardy, heady, and accomplished, James was every inch a Scot, and fit to be a king of Scots.

4. The nobles of his kingdom, many of them poor and proud, with thoughts too high for their restricted fortunes, were compelled to follow him for largess. Civil strife had cut down many a duke and earl, and James had the disposal of these ancient fiefs. Four duchies graced the Scottish crown. Of these four duchies three were vacant, and the fourth was held by Ross, a younger brother of the King. Twenty-five earldoms graced that crown; of which no less than nine were vacant, and two were held by a second brother of the King. The crown was therefore rich in fiefs, although so poor in coin that James had more than once to melt the chalice from his table and the collar from his neck. Intriguers were at work on every side of him. High dignities were only to be got from James through fear and favour; daunting him by frown of armed men, and dazzling him by light of lovely eyes. The Humes and Hepburns tried the first; the Kennedeys and Drummonds tried the second. Each and all succeeded in their quest.

5. Sir John Drummond placed his daughter, known in song as "Bonnie Margaret," in James's way. The house of Drummond had already given a queen to Scotland. Drummond was connected with the highest families, but not a member of those families tried to snatch his daughter from the King. The rough old Pictish ways were common, and at Stirling Castle no one dreamt of saying that an amour with the King was wrong. In every country-house, the monarch found bewitching women and complacent knights. Sir John became Lord Drummond of Stobhall, on the River Tay, and afterwards of Drummond Castle in the valley of Strathearn. Bonnie Margaret bore the King a daughter, whom he openly adopted as his child. Accepted as a member of the royal house, this daughter of Bonnie Margaret lived to marry the Earl of Huntly; but her mother held no undisputed reign. Mary Boyd allured the King away, and in a fit of penitence, James returned his favourite to her home, and married her to another man. This rival bore the King a son, Alexander, who was afterwards Archbishop of St. Andrews, and a daughter, Catharine, who lived to marry James, third Earl of Morton. In his fit of penitence, he also married Mary Boyd to one who offered her his hand. "The King gave up his love-making," says Ayala, "as well from fear of God as fear of worldly scandal, which is very much thought of here." But James was soon himself again. James Stuart, Earl of Buchan, had a daughter, Lady Isobel, who found some favour in her kinsman's eyes. She bore a daughter, Janet, to her royal lover, and retained an interest in his

heart for many years. The former favourite, Bonnie Margaret, was recalled, and Drummond reappeared at court. "They favour his intrigues," Ayala wrote in reference to the Scottish nobles, "in order to subject him to their will."

6. Kennedey, Earl of Cassilis, being jealous of these Drummonds, who were boasting that the King would marry Bonnie Margaret, induced his daughter, Lady Janet Kennedey, to try and steal away his heart. This Janet, lovely and unscrupulous as a witch, had flung away her maiden fame before she knew the King, and lived a life of shame with that Archibald, Earl of Angus, who was known at court as Archibald Bell-the-Cat. She lay in wait for James as he was going on a pilgrimage to St. Ninian's shrine; a favourite time and place for carrying out her father's plot. She carried off the prize, and Margaret lost her empire in the King. This wicked Lady Janet reigned a longer time than any other woman, saving gentle Lady Isobel. Her children, James and Janet, bore the royal name of Stuart, and the royal castle of Dernaway was settled on her while she lived entirely for the King.

7. A strange event—a mystery, if not a murder—brought the flood of passion for his early favourite, Bonnie Margaret, back to James, but in a form to chasten and subdue the wanderings of his life. That lady, being at Drummond Castle, with her sisters, Sybil and Euphemia, was at the breakfast-table, when she felt a curious qualm. She rose from table. She was ill. Her sisters rose; they too were ill. No leech could do them good. At dawn they were

in perfect health; at sundown all the three were dead. Much haste was made to get them under ground; their uncle, Walter, Dean of Dunblane, removing their remains from Drummond Castle where they died, and burying them in his cathedral, where their ashes could not be disturbed by order of a secular judge. The King was stunned. No clue has yet been caught by which the mystery can be traced. The Kennedeys were long suspected of the deed, and Janet's witcheries could not clear away the doubt from James's mind. He fetched his child by Bonnie Margaret to Stirling Castle, and he paid for daily masses to be said and sung in the cathedral for his favourite's soul.

Such were the country and the man for whom the Scottish envoys were to offer peace and to prepare a match.

CHAPTER VI.

Margaret's Betrothal.

1502.

1. OUTSIDE the city wall, among the trees and swards of Clerkenwell, arose an abbey church, with belfry that arrested every eye, and carried the attention of a stranger from the tower and pinnacle of St. Paul's. The abbey stood on rising ground, above the River Fleet; the belfry, though of English shape, was graven, gilded, and enamelled in the richest Oriental style. From every height round London that imposing church and shining belfry could be seen, and he who caught the radiance was enjoined to turn in reverence towards the Holy Land, and pray that God, in His good time, would heal those schisms in the Christian commonwealth which gave the grave of Christ into the power of infidels and Turks. Around this abbey church were grouped the buildings of a great religious order, that of the Knights-hospitallers of Jerusalem, whose special patron was St. John. Among these buildings were a prior's house, a hostelry for guests, a farm, a court, a burying-place, and lodgings for a regiment of knights. These piles were rich in story as in aspect. Founded by Count de Briset in the days of Godfrey de Boulogne, the abbey had been con-

secrated by Heraclius, Patriarch of Jerusalem, and burnt to ashes in the times of Cade. Rebuilt by many patrons—for the monkish knights were high in favour, and especially with noble dames—the priory became a sort of royal court, where princes came to lodge and councils met on state affairs. This priory had been connected in a special manner with the Henries. Under Henry the First it had been built. Here Henry the Second had received the messengers of Baldwin, King of Jerusalem, who came to offer him an Eastern crown. Here Henry the Third had lodged his daughter-in-law, Elinor of Castille. The fourth and fifth Henrys had both resided in the priory of St. John. Nor was the reigning Henry minded to forget this hospital. Since his accession, he had sought to make the Prior a personal friend and counsellor, and he was busy with a plan for adding to the size and beauty of the abbey church.

2. While the ambassadors from James were on the road, his Prior, Father Kendal, died. The Prior's house was empty, and the King, in his desire to do these envoys courtesy, lodged them in this home of kings. A dry and healthy place, though rich in wood and water, was the monastery of St. John. A river bathed the garden slopes. Green meadows lay in front; the noble convent of St. Mary stood behind. Two great monastic houses, Charter House and St. Bartholomew, lay between them and the city wall. The priory was a palace, and connected, in remembrance with a former King of Scots. Here Alexander, when a Prince, had been

received by John, and knighted at the Prior's board. In every way the Scottish ministers were fittingly and nobly lodged.

3. Deane, Archbishop of Canterbury, Fox, Bishop of Winchester, and Thomas, Earl of Surrey, were appointed a commission to confer with Blacater, Forman, and Bothwell, on the terms and details of the match. Much riding to and from the priory was needed, for the matters to be settled by these agents were of many kinds. Grave councillors urged objections to the match on principle. The English lines might fail, in which event the English crown would go to Lady Margaret's son. That son would be a Scot in birth and training, and the kingdom would become an appanage of the northern crown. These words amused the King, who studied policy as a science. "If the thing you fear should come to pass," he answered, "England would annex Scotland, for the greater always draws the less." To every one who, urged by ancient rancour, spoke against the Scots, he said, "It is a safer match than that of France." Some pride of place came in to cause delay. The English councillors insisted on a declaration that the King of Scots had begged and prayed for Lady Margaret, and that the King, her father, had with much ado been brought to grant his suit. The Scots endeavoured to avoid this plea. There were disputes about the dowry, the establishment, the journey, and the time of marriage; and the Scottish agents needed some repose among the tombs of ancient knights, and in an atmosphere of monks and nuns.

4. But they were not allowed to live among these tombs of ancient knights, and in this atmosphere of monks and nuns. A younger world came knocking at their door and asking to be made a partner in their toils. This younger world was of the Boleyn stamp; new men, enriched by trade and enterprise; the citizens of Cheape and Lombard Street, who cared but little for the tombs of ancient knights, and nothing for an atmosphere of living monks and nuns. The City knights were not then carpet knights. In forty years no less than fifteen Lord Mayors had been knighted on the field. John Shaw, whose term had just expired, had been created knight and banneret by a sovereign sparing of rewards. Yet they were men who loved to sheathe the sword, and hang the firelock on its rack. If an invader pressed the soil, the City bands were ready to go out, but they had no desire to harry and destroy the border shires. The world had grown too vast for these old feuds and thefts. A herd of kine was nothing, and the plunder of a town not much, to men who were engaged in opening ports from Cuba to Cathay. Their hopes were with Columbus in his caravels. They talked of Pinzon, Cabot, and De Gama. They were brisk with work and trade, and spent their energies in building ships, in selling produce, and in settling desert lands. Alert and open to ideas, they were listeners in their leisure hours to men like Wycliffe, and the City wards in which these merchants lived were hated by the monks and priests as strongholds of the Bible-men.

5. A good example of his class, Bartholomew Rede, Lord Mayor, invited the commissioners to a City feast. Like Capel, Coke, and Jocelyn, his immediate neighbours, Rede was an example of a class who filled their coffers, founded schools, and executed public works. Rede built a free school in his native town, and many of his fellows in the City spent a portion of their wealth on public works. Hugh Clopton (owner of the "great house" in which Shakespeare afterwards lived and died) built a fine stone bridge at Stratford on the Avon. William Fitzwilliam built a great part of St. Andrew Undershaft. Stephen Jennings built the grammar-school at Wolverhampton. Henry Kebble gave a hundred and forty ploughs to husbandmen in Oxfordshire and Warwickshire. William Coffinger left half his huge estates to the poor. John Saxe built the hospital of St. Antony's Church. A son of Colet was the founder of St. Paul's School. Jocelyn was a Knight of the Bath; Fitzwilliam a Privy Councillor. But much of their renown was still to come. These men were all to have illustrious progeny. Capel was ancestor of the Earl of Essex and the Marquis of Winchester; Coke, of Lord Bacon, of the Marquis of Salisbury, and the Marquis of Exeter; Jocelyn, of the Earl of Roden. Misfine, skinner, was the grandfather of John Hampden and Oliver Cromwell. Locke, a younger man, but soon to take his freedom, was the ancestor of John Locke, of Chancellor King, and of the Earl of Lovelace. Rede, the new Lord Mayor, had come from Norfolk, entered on the goldsmith's craft, amassed a

fortune, and been knighted by the King. Four years ago he served as sheriff, and became the alderman of Cheape. In prospect of the civic chain, he purchased Crosby Place, not long since occupied by Richard, and in this historic palace, he received and entertained his Scottish guests. Dunbar repaid the citizens for meat and wine by the delivery of an Ode, in which he spoke of London as the flower of cities, of her business men as royal merchants, and her dames as lovesome, small, and fair.

6. At length the treaty was arranged. The dowry was thirty thousand golden nobles. Lady Margaret was to have five hundred marks a-year as pin-money, and a jointure, which the King her husband was to manage, of two thousand pounds a-year in rent. On Monday, January the twenty-fourth, the festival of St. Cadoc, an assembly met at Richmond, where the two bodies of commissioners signed a permanent and solemn league of peace between the crowns. In one respect, the Scots were disappointed in their hope. They had imagined Henry would restore to them the town of Berwick; but the King would never listen to this suit; and they were fain to either drop the question or return as they had come. They dropt it. On the following day, the festival of St. Paul, the temporal and spiritual peers assembled in the chapel. Mass was said, and Richard, Bishop of Rochester, preached a sermon. Then the King and Queen, accompanied by the Duke of York and Lady Mary, led Ayala and the Scottish messengers, followed by a crowd of pre-

lates, peers, and knights, into the Queen's hall, where Bothwell, lay ambassador, stood as proxy for his lord. The ceremony of espousals was performed, on which a blare of trumpets from the leads told every one in Richmond that the Lady Margaret was henceforth Queen of Scots.

CHAPTER VII.

Ludlow Castle.

1502.

1. ATTENDED by the Bishop of Lincoln and the Lords of Council, Arthur and Catharine entered Ludlow early in the year. Received with rapture by the townfolk, who were proud to see their prince, they entered the baronial hall prepared for them by Henry's care. A place still dear to lovers of romantic scenery and noble verse, this border castle stands on rising ground, some part of which lies backward in the town, and covered by the wall, but much of it runs forward on a rocky bluff, and overhangs a limpid stream. Below this strong embattled front the Corve flows into the Teme, through soft and verdant breadths of flat and slope. Corve Dale, with all her beauties, lay beneath their eyes. A wooded hill rose up beyond these pastures, and a rolling landscape led the mind away to distant mountain chains. This castle has a striking place in the great drama of our history. Built by Roger de Montgomery, it was seized by Henry the First, besieged in vain by Stephen, stormed and carried by De Montfort, made a rendezvous by Richard Plantagenet, Duke of York. Nor was the castle wanting in poetic memories. Ludlow had been the

scene of Marian's wild revenge; the home of Roger Mortimer, the guilty partner of Queen Elinor; a property of the De Lacies; and a home of Edward, the unfortunate Prince of Wales, who left it for his chamber in the Bloody Tower.

2. In this romantic seat the Prince and Princess held a court at which the knights and gentry of the border shires were welcomed with a round of tilts and feasts, when Catharine, though she could not speak their language, crowned the victors with her eyes and hands. Sir Richard Pole took care the girl should be amused, and Bishop Smyth induced the boy to give his mornings to affairs of state. The Prince had much to do in Wales beyond reviving Camelot and her wandering knights. Fierce passions were alive around him, and on every side he found dark traces of the havoc wrought by civil strife. Ludlow was a ruined town. Delivered by the chance of war into Lancastrian hands, the houses had been ravaged to the walls. What could be eaten had been swallowed up; what could be stolen had been swept away; what could be merely burnt had been set on fire. The castle had been roughly spoiled, but Edward, in his day of vengeance, had been able to redress all injuries done to property of his crown. Much might be done by princely words to quicken the repair of what was ruined; and the Prince, amidst his masks and revels, gave a ready ear and warm encouragement to every one who wrought his best at building, planting, and repairing the old border town.

4. Two months after bride and groom had

ridden out of London, Henry wrote a letter to the King and Queen of Spain, in which he told them what was done, and hinted, in a general way, that in allowing Catharine to go down to Ludlow Castle, he was carrying out their wishes, not his own. The plate was nowhere mentioned; but his hints of long debates in council, of the opposition of many peers and prelates, of the sudden resolution taken by the King to let her go, seemed meant to check complaints. His letter ran:

"To the most serene and most puissant Prince and Princess the Lord and Lady Fernando and Isabel, by the Grace of God King and Queen of Castille, Leon, Aragon, Sicily, Granada, etc., our well-beloved kinsfolk and cousins, we Henry, by the same grace King of England and France, and Lord of Ireland, send greeting and ever-increasing good fortune. That we might observe the ancient customs of our realm, we recently despatched into Wales the most illustrious Arthur and Catharine, our common children. For although the opinions of many were adverse to this course by reason of the tender age of our son, yet were we unwilling to allow the prince and princess to be separated at any distance from each other. Thus much we wished to show unto you by this our letter, that you may understand our excessive love which we bear towards the most illustrious Lady Catharine, our common daughter, even to the danger of our own son. But the said most illustrious lady has with her a venerable man, Alessandro Geraldino, her principal chaplain, for whom we have the greatest regard, partly by reason of his virtues shown unto us in many ways, and partly because he has been the said lady's preceptor, and for a long time your Highnesses' servant. And we doubt not that he will, in his letters, give a true report unto your Highnesses of the well-being and tranquillity as well of ourselves and our realm as of the most illustrious lady his own mistress. Wherefore we shall not at present write at greater length. From our castle of Richmond, this 20th day of February, 1501-2.

"HENRY R."

Secreted at a later date, this letter lay for centuries in a private cabinet of the kings of Spain.

4. The rough old border people liked the Prince, whose grace and gentleness were of daily use in softening family feuds and party strife. An air of youth was in his court. Ludlow began to smile again. The streets were cleared, the houses built afresh. New shops were opened in the town; but these material changes were the least in Arthur's eyes. He set himself the highest task on earth,— to succour and defend the poor who could not help themselves. A cruel war had not been worse to them than cruel laws. On searching through the border code he found the laws in use a mere chaotic mass. A few were obsolete; still more were useless; and the rest were mischievous. His council, most of whom were Welsh, as Philips, Udal, Crofts, and Vernon, took the local code in hand, for an oppressive law is worse than an imperious chief. Reform was pressed by Bishop Smyth in council,

while the Prince was steadily at work within his household. Arthur strove to put down private brawls, but rather by the precept of a gentle life than by the exercise of regal strength. If any one bore malice, Arthur would not own him. If a courtier had a quarrel, Arthur searched into the cause, and took the part of him whose course was just. A keen observer of the boy at Ludlow said of him, "He sought to strengthen and preserve the law, and gave his soul and body to the service of Almighty God."

5. While Arthur was engaged in Camelot on these knightly tasks, a new disease broke out, which the physician, Bereworth, fancied was a form of plague. Much rain had lately fallen in the Shropshire hills. Elvira found the climate damp, and Catharine, used to southern sunshine, shivered in the marshy meads and dripping woods. Fernando heard that Ludlow was a dull, unwholesome town, as in the rainy months it must have seemed to men and women fresh from the Alhambra gardens, where the citron is in bloom and fruit the whole year round. The Prince caught cold, and could not shake it off. In spite of Bereworth's care he sank, as in a falling sickness. No one knew of what he ailed. Some called his sickness waste, while others called it plague. One thing alone was clear; the boy was dying in his teens; and that so fast, that Pole could send for neither Queen nor King in time to see him die. The girl, not five months married, was alone with him, in that strange place, without a mother to advise her, and a cham-

berlain and doctor in her husband's chamber whom she could not understand. Had she but known a little French, she might have been a comfort to the Prince. But an interpreter at a dying bed, translating gasp and sigh from English into Latin and from Latin into Castillian, was a task too weary to go on from day to day. She could do nothing for him but retire. The boy and girl were parted by their fates. When Arthur called his notaries and made his will, he seemed to have forgotten the fair woman who had recently become his wife. He thought of others, who were nearer to his heart. In these last moments of his life on earth, he turned to that fond sister who had been his playmate as a child, and who was now contracted to the King of Scots. To Margaret he left his cups and rings, his robes and household stuff.

On Saturday, the second day of April, he expired—the shadowy prince whom men had called too good to live.

6. A child, a widow, and a stranger in that border town, with no one save a chaplain and some women to advise her, Catharine felt that failing of the heart which sometimes overtakes the bravest men; and going to her chamber in the Castle, with her faithful maid, Maria de Salazar, she shut her door in Moorish fashion on the world; devolving the sad duties of her house on Pole, the chamberlain, who sent off letters with his awful message to the King and Queen.

CHAPTER VIII.

At Greenwich.

1502.

1. By the water-side of Greenwich, where the river curls about the Isle of Dogs, a royal lodge had stood in ancient days. The spot was lovely, and commanded landscapes lovelier than itself. Green swards ran upward to the crown of two fine hills, and in the dip between these heights lay many a clump of venerable trees. A fleet of ships adorned the river, and a herd of deer adorned the park. A castle, built by good Duke Humphrey, crowned the greater height, and in this castle Mary of York, a sister of the Queen, had lived and died. The lodge beside the water had been called the Plaisaunce, but the good Duke Humphrey, on repairing it, had changed the name from Plaisaunce to Placentia. Henry liked the spot, and as the Queen, to whom it bore a memory of her sister, liked it also, he enlarged the pile, rebuilt the river front, threw up some cells for his attendant friars, and made Placentia a retreat from his abounding cares of state.

2. At Greenwich, Henry, Duke of York, was born, and as the Duke was more robust than any other of the royal infants, Greenwich was supposed to have a wholesome air. When Lady Margaret

had been promised to the King of Scots, and the commissioners had left for Stirling, every one content in heart, the King and Queen had dropt to Greenwich with their children, to enjoy those days of privacy which Henry loved so well.

3. Pole's messengers arrived at Greenwich in the dead of Monday night, all splashed and grimy from their rapid ride. The lights were out, the King was gone to bed. But news like Pole's will hardly keep. A councillor was found, who sent an officer to call his colleagues of the board. Awakened from their sleep, these councillors hurried to the chamber, and perused the letter out of Wales. What man would break this message to the King? Too well they knew his dread lest all his masculine line should fail. Of three sons whom the Queen had borne him two were gone. The future seemed to hang upon a thread. What words of comfort could a councillor use? It was no case of private grief. Prince Arthur's death exposed the nation to a second civil war. Nor were the females stronger than the males. Lady Elizabeth, the King's second daughter, lay in Westminster Abbey. Lady Mary, next in age, was delicate in health. What could the wisest of his councillors say?

4. In seeking right and left for some one who might break these tidings to the King, they thought of an Observant friar who lived hard by, in one of those poor sheds which Henry had erected on the river bank. For him they sent, and after showing him the news from Pole, they begged him, as a man of God, to whom his Grace would listen with

respect, to go and tell him what had come to pass. This friar, who was the King's confessor, knew his duty, and might speak to him in tones no other man would dare to use. He bowed his head, accepted his commission, and retired till it was time to go into the room and speak. Before the night was past, he stole into the corridor where Henry slept, and tapping at the door, as he was wont to do when coming on his ghostly errands, listened for an answering voice within. A voice within the room asked who was there so early in the day? "It is I, the King's confessor," he replied. The pages let him in. "Leave us alone," he whispered, as he passed these youths, and having cleared the room, he turned a sad face towards the King and said: "Si bona de manu Dei suscipimus, mala autem quare non sustineamus?" Then he told his grace, that Arthur, Prince of Wales, was gone to God.

5. "Send some one for the Queen," gasped Henry, stricken to the heart, "and let me bear this grief with her." The Queen came in, and seeing how her husband reeled and sank beneath this blow, she tried to comfort him, as wife and queen should do in such a loss. Too well she saw where he was pierced, and how the shaft struck home. Not only was his boy gone from him, but his heir was dead. The day-dream of his life had melted into mist. King Arthur and his court were henceforth to be only found in song, and even the relapse of England into civil war might turn upon the chances of a single life. If Henry, Duke of York, should also fail, the house of Lancaster would be left without a

prince, and either Pole or Courtney might be chosen to succeed the King. In brief, the sceptre would return from Lancaster to York. She knew what chord to strike in Henry's heart, and looking up into his face, she bade him dwell on what was left to them, as well as pine for what was lost. It was for God, she said, to give, for God to take away. One life might prove as good as twenty lives. His mother, he should bear in mind, had but one son, yet he, that only son, was there and on his throne. His life was spared, his cause was blessed, his crown was won. All men regarded him as one of the wisest and most prosperous kings on earth. If much was taken from them, see how much remained! They had a fine young prince, and two princesses, to renew their line. Nor were they yet too old for hope. She was but thirty-five years old, and God might give them other sons. His grace, she urged, should think of her a little, of himself still more, and of his country most of all. At length, he rallied to her voice. He raised his eyes to look on her, so beautiful and strong. He felt the beauty of her love, and stilled for her the passion and despair which tore his inmost heart. When he seemed easy in his mind, she softly left his side, and crept away in silence to her room.

6. Some minutes later he was called in haste to her apartments. She was swooning on her bed, and he who had been soothed and strengthened by her words, had now to calm and cheer the mother who had lost her son. In these sad moments of bereavement love was paid by love. On both sides,

it was, "Let me bear this grief with her," and "Let me bear this grief with him!" And thus, in the retreat which they had built for love and privacy, the King and Queen of England mourned in silence for their first-born son.

BOOK THE EIGHTH.

CATHARINE'S PARENTS.

CHAPTER I.

Toledo.

1502.

1. At midnight, on the tenth of May, the King and Queen of Spain were seated in a dim and lofty chamber of the Moorish palace at Toledo, trying to unlock the secrets of a short despatch. That evening messengers had swept across the bridge and up the ramp-like streets. They brought a note in cypher, brief in words, but full of menace for the Court. At length the King and Queen had made the cyphers yield their story. Catharine, so lately gone from them in bridal hope, was now a widow in a foreign land. Like Isabel, her sister, she had tasted in her teens the bitterness of death. Her situation in that border town, with a dead husband, and without a friend to guide her steps, was one to touch a heart of bronze. A child, a widow — she was little over sixteen years of age. She could not understand the speech of Pole and Smyth. Her

native councillors, Fonseca, Cabra, and their mates, were gone away. Her native servants had been lowered in rank. Except her foreign chaplain, Padre Alessandro, not a man was near to whom she could apply for counsel. In her misery she was utterly alone. Yet not one word of love and greeting left the capital of Castille that night! Her parents had no time to waste on words of love. Their game was checked. By Arthur's death their purpose in her marriage had been foiled; just as their purpose in her sister's union with Affonzo had been foiled. A Dowager Princess of Wales could neither wear the English crown, nor govern those who might be called to wear that English crown.

2. They bade their secretary, Almazan, take up his pen and write. A man of confidence must be chosen and despatched to London, where a work was to be done for Spain that priests like Alessandro and lawyers like Puebla could not touch. The business was so weighty that the usual forms of etiquette must be set aside. A man of rank must go; a man of highest rank and nearest trust; for he would have to act with the authority and confidence of a king. The agent whom they wanted lay in an adjoining room. Estrada, chamberlain and councillor, was a personal friend, a duke in rank, and one of the oldest officers in their court. He knew their secrets and their projects. Should a doubt arise, he knew their mind, and could be trusted with their seal. But not a moment could be lost. Affairs were at the turning-point; he must be gone ere break of day; and he must travel by the shortest roads.

Five weeks had passed away since Arthur died, and who could say what plots were now afloat? The French were never slow, and they had just then reason for the hottest haste. A new and deadly war was opening in the South; a war that would decide the fate of Italy, and give to either France or Spain a virtual primacy of the West. French troops, they knew, were marching through the Alps; French agents, they were sure, were flocking to the Thames. Estrada ought to be in London by the end of May. So striking an event as Arthur's sudden death might justify the Duke in asking leave to go through France, even though the countries were so near a rupture that the Queen was listening daily for the guns. Estrada could be told by word of mouth what he would have to do and say when he arrived in London, but he ought to leap to horse that night, and get to England ere the mischief had been done. Let him depart at once, not waiting for his papers and credentials, which would take some hours to frame, translate, and sign.

3. One scrap of paper, which was signed by both the King and Queen, was put into Estrada's hand. That scrap of paper was addressed to Puebla, telling him that Duke Estrada was ambassador extraordinary, putting every one in Catharine's household under his control, and bidding them obey the royal chamberlain as though he were both King and Queen of Spain.

4. At no time had a close connexion with the English Court appeared of so much moment to the King and Queen as now. If war should come,

they could not look to Germany for help against the French. Since Juan's death, the Austrian league had proved to them, by turns a trap, a fetter, and a curse. Juana's husband, Philip, had his word in every council, and his partizan in every street. His son, an Austrian prince, was heir; and they were feeling all the bitterness of their dependence on a man like Kaiser Max. Not long ago the penniless Emperor had borrowed forty thousand florins from the King of Naples, who had lent this money on condition that the Emperor should refuse to sign a truce with France. But Louis, a more subtle schemer than his predecessor Charles, had tempted Max with heaps of ducats; and Max, without repaying Federigo any of his money, had signed a truce and left the road to Naples open to the French. In turn, the King and Queen of Spain had sought once more to square accounts with France. This time their task had not been hard; for George d'Amboise, Cardinal of Rouen, chief friend and minister of Louis, had an eye upon the Papal chair, and hoped by pleasing them to gain the Spanish vote in Rome. Amboise had counselled Louis to accept proposals for dividing Naples, and the infamous Treaty of Granada had been signed; by which Louis and Fernando undertook to conquer and divide between them Federigo's kingdom, and to guarantee each other in possession of their spoil. Two armies, under Nemours and Gonsalvo, had been thrown into the country, and as Italy was rent by factions, and Cesare Borgia, priest and fratricide, had joined the foreigners, success had waited on their arms. Federigo had been driven from Naples and his dynasty uncrowned.

5. But when these conquerors had come to share the plunder, they had not been able to agree. Apulia and Calabria had been seized by Spain; Campagna and Abruzzi had been occupied by France. Some districts of the country were disputed, and the generals, allies of a day, had carried these disputes with overbearing pride. Nemours had required Gonsalvo to withdraw his troops beyond a certain line. Gonsalvo had replied to these demands by fortifying several towns. In Paris, Nemours' haughty language was approved. His means being greater than Gonsalvo's, the French imagined they could drive the Spaniards to their ships and keep the country for themselves. All France was arming. Louis had departed for his camp, and troops were pouring into Languedoc. A furious war was issuing from a monstrous treaty; yet at this decisive hour, when Spain was closing in a hug of mortal strife with France, the tie which bound the courts of London and Granada to pursue a common policy in Europe, had been snapt by Arthur's death! At any cost, those ties must be renewed.

6. Estrada having ridden away, the King and Queen prepared two papers of instructions for his guidance, which the secretary was to send as soon as they could be engrossed and sealed. The first of these two papers was a public letter, which Estrada was to show the Tudor king in council; while the second was a private letter, which he was to show the King in secret. By his public com-

mission Estrada was empowered, as envoy from the King and Queen of Spain, to claim from Henry, in their joint and several names, and in the name of Catharine, prompt repayment of the hundred thousand crowns, and a conveyance of the manors, rents, and goods assigned to Catharine at St. Paul's. He was to add, that Catharine must be sent to Spain, that Henry must provide the necessary ships, and that the whole expenses of her journey must be paid by England. By his secret commission, he was authorized to propose a league between the crowns of Spain and England, for their mutual aid; a league which was to be cemented by a match between the Spanish widow and her English brother-in-law, the Duke of York. Full explanations went along with these two formal papers, so that nothing might be left in doubt. The royal orders were that he should push the business of his mission at his utmost speed. He was to suffer no delay, and settle every point the moment it arose. No questions as to either dowry, plate, or jewels, were to stay him. Nay, he was not asked to write, except when he could say that everything was done, and Catharine was contracted to the Duke of York.

7. Such were the plots begun that night in the old Moorish palace at Toledo: plots that were to wreck their daughter's life, and help to rend the Universal Church. Before they heard how Catharine had been left, before they spoke one word of Arthur's death, the King and Queen of Spain had taken all these measures to provide a second marriage of their daughter to an English prince. Their

project was so strange that nothing can excuse, and nothing short of stern necessity can explain it. Both the King and Queen were well aware that Catharine was a sister-in-law of Henry, Duke of York. In every word they recognised this fact of facts. They called their daughter the Princess of Wales. They paid her dowry as Princess of Wales. They claimed her settlements as Princess of Wales. Yet no consideration for their daughter, for society, and for religion, stayed their hands. A war was opening, and they wanted Catharine on the English throne.

CHAPTER II.

New Proposals.

1502.

1. Two days elapsed before the King and Queen of Spain found time to think of Catharine as their child. When the instructions to Estrada had been signed and sealed, they wrote a line to Puebla, which they told him he must show to every one he met. Their hearts, they wrote, were drowned by his sad news, and yet in humble piety they bowed their heads. The will of God must be obeyed. They grieved to hear that Catharine was unwell; the town she dwelt in was, they heard, unwholesome; and the King, their brother, should be asked to move her to some fitting place. It was the sort of letter their Italian scribe was paid for writing. Not a word was said about Estrada's journey and the object of his going to the English court. Their hearts were full of love and care. They wanted news, fresh news, and ever more fresh news. They bade their envoy write, and write, and send them messages by sea and land.

2. Puebla wrote and sent too soon. Not guessing that his King and Queen were plotting for a second match in London, and supposing they were anxious as to Catharine's jointure, he enclosed a

piece of evidence which was to set their minds at rest. He knew that if a doubt arose about the marriage being an actual marriage, Warham, as a lawyer, might object to pay. The letter he enclosed was one from Alessandro, Catharine's chaplain, stating in the simplest words that Catharine was a lawful widow of the Prince, and therefore could not be refused the payment of her jointure as the Dowager Princess of Wales.

3. A month ago, they would have given the canonist a mitre for this news, but Arthur's death had upset all their schemes, and in their sudden change of policy it might be well to leave that problem in the shade. Their fears now led them to adopt a theory of their daughter's married life more fitted for the comic stage than for a serious board. In dealing with the question of her settlements, they argued that she was Prince Arthur's widow; while in dealing with the question of her second marriage, they contended she had never been his wife. Estrada's two commissions showed these opposite sides: the public letter speaking of Catharine only as Princess of Wales; the private letter only as Lady Catharine, daughter of the King and Queen of Spain. They would have liked to keep both courses open, and to choose their line according to events. But Puebla's note compelled them to review the situation, and decide what language they would hold in Catharine's house.

4. The English people stood on texts. No Spaniard would have cared whether Catharine had been married to the Prince or not, because the

Spaniards held that no impediment to marriage was beyond the faculty of Rome to set aside. Few English people had such confidence in the Roman court. One school of canonists in Rome contended that the Papal privilege of dispensing with the penalties incurred by sin was absolute. Less courtly lawyers, even near the Vatican, held that this high privilege was limited by Holy Scripture; but the favourite lawyers of the Pontiff held that his dispensing power was absolute, both in kind and in extent. It was admitted that a Pope could only use this faculty for the public good, in urgent cases, and when ordinary methods of relief had failed; but he was held to be the judge of what was for the public good, of when a state of urgency arose, of whether all the ordinary methods had been tried. A right thus limited was hardly limited at all. The Spaniards, as a nation, held these courtly views of the dispensing power. Not many English priests and people shared these views. They sought a higher law elsewhere, and found that Papal powers were limited by the law of God. The Spanish King and Queen were driven to make a choice, and as the marriage was of more importance than the money, they resolved, though they might lose her settlements by the avowal, to declare that Catharine was a merely nominal Princess of Wales. Estrada must be warned in time. Before he landed he might hear some rumour, and should have his answer on his lips. He was to treat the rumour as the tattle of a priest. If any one should mention Puebla as a witness, he must hint that Puebla, like the chaplain, had some object of his own in view. To stop all further chatter, they directed him to put a curb on every tongue in Catharine's house, from that of her chamberlain to that of her cook or sweep.

5. Two persons, however, Puebla and Alessandro, held their secret, who were not so easily curbed yet. Puebla, they imagined, might be trusted, since his wages and his safety lay in prompt submission to their will. He was a Spaniard, and his family lived in Spain. Though Henry had been talking of his settlement in London, with either a wealthy widow for a wife, or some fat canonry for a consolation, nothing had been done for him as yet. He was a Spanish subject, open to recall and punishment. If he refused to come, they had a weapon in reserve. He had a daughter living in his house at Seville; they had an inquisitor lodging in their castle at Triana. Not a mile divided Puebla's house from Isabel's castle. By a secret sign this girl might be denounced; no proofs of guilt would be required; and familiars from Triana would soon be rioting in the envoy's house. What came of seizure by Dominicans he had seen. His daughter might be whisked away; his goods and chattels might be carted off. The woman might be lost. No secular judge could seek her out; no secular eye would see her face; by fasting, darkness, torture, and despair, she might be driven to say and sign whatever she was asked to say and sign. That all this could be done with her was not long after put to proof.

6. But Alessandro was another man. He was no Spanish subject. An Italian, he was not com-

pelled by family interests to return. A priest, he was an upright man; a soldier, he was frank and bold; a foreigner, he was free to speak the truth. Attached to Catharine as her teacher and confessor, he was likely to consider what was good for her, before he thought of what might turn out good for him; and hence the King and Queen were much afraid that when their project came to light, this faithful priest might warn their daughter in his spiritual office that a union with her husband's brother would be mortal sin. They dared not trust him; yet to get him back into their power was not an easy task. If Alessandro were in Spain, he could be forced to hold his tongue, and should Estrada fail to satisfy him that his view was wrong, they saw he must be got on board a ship, and brought immediately to Spain. A copy of his note was therefore sent in cypher to Estrada, with minute instructions for his guidance in this nice affair. No pother must be raised. Estrada was to read the note, and keep the contents to himself. He was to ask Elvira what she knew, and what was known to others. Not a whisper must be breathed to Catharine on the subject. Alessandro must be treated with respect, as one whom they were pleased to honour, but he must not hear that they had seen his note. In what was further to be done, Estrada should be guided by Elvira. If the priest were likely to do harm, he must be got away; but things must be arranged so wisely that he would not guess the cause of his return to Spain. "Be on your guard," they wrote, "in order that what is being said shall do no harm, when in God's good pleasure the marriage has been finally arranged."

7. As such an offer was unlikely to be well received in London, they considered how to work on Henry's mind. He was a thrifty man. The comedy of Catharine's plate had shown them how he might be swayed by love of gold. As only one instalment of the dowry had been paid, he had been asking for his second store of crowns. They met this claim by a refusal, and by something worse than a refusal of the money. They affected to believe that Arthur's death had thrown a great advantage into Catharine's lap. The Prince had made on her a settlement of a third of his estate. His death, they said, had left that settlement untouched, while Catharine's dowry must return with her to Spain! The law, they said, was clear. To fortify their plea, they laid a case before the University of Salamanca, where in due time and at some expense, they got opinions from the doctors in their favour, which they sent to England, and submitted to the King. All means, direct and indirect, were taken to convince the thrifty monarch that unless he married Catharine to his younger son, he would sustain in her a grievous loss.

8. Ere long Fernando found this business much too nice for his direct and masculine style of treatment, and, engrossed with his affairs in Italy and France, he gave the English charge to Isabel, his wife, who thenceforth took the leading part in forcing Catharine on the Duke of York.

CHAPTER III.

Durham House.

1502.

1. Lodged in her private room at Ludlow, with her maids of honour and her native servants, Catharine took no part in the poetic obsequies of her lord. Three weeks he lay in state where he had died, with lighted tapers, darkened rooms, funereal black and white, a princely crown, emblazoned shield and arms, monks, watchers, yeomen of the guard, sad silence, solemn knells, the chant of nones and vespers, and the whole array and pomp of a majestic grief. All forms that sorrow could invent were lavished on the boy. "Spare nothing," said the King and Queen. A resting-place was chosen for him in the Cathedral of Worcester, in the chancel, on the right-hand side. Sir Reginald Bray was asked to build a chapel and a tomb. The road from Ludlow to Worcester, running through a length of dales and forests, had been roughened by the rains, yet every chapel on that road was turned into a shrine. At every shrine, the cavalcade was halted, and a solemn mass was said. At Bewdley, on the Severn, there was longer pause, for Bewdley was a royal manor, and a favourite hunting-lodge. At Bewdley, Arthur had espoused his bride by proxy, and on his return to Bewdley

dead, his bride was only at his side by proxy. Mass was chanted for his soul, and then the sad procession moved to Worcester, where, amid the sobs and tears of a whole nation, Arthur of Winchester was laid beneath the chancel wall. A shadow he had come, a shadow he was gone.

2. The Queen, though broken by her grief, had time to think of Catharine in her lonely state. She sent for Cope, her tailor, and desired him to prepare a litter, black with crape and velvet, as became a mourning bride, and when the thing was made, she sent for Catharine up to London, where she welcomed her with tender love. Along the road from Ludlow, she was everywhere received with royal honours, as the lady next in station to the Queen. Her face was sad and strange; but not with the strange sadness of a breaking heart. Such griefs as snap the cords of life were not for girls so young in years, so warm in blood, so flush in temper as the Spanish lady. On the road, her rank as princess was conceded; no one in her court, and no one in the country, dreaming that she was a merely nominal widow of the Prince. The King, though eager to secure his dynasty from risks, put off, on good advice, the ceremony of creating his second son a Prince of Wales. Forty-three weeks elapsed before he ventured to confer this honour on his son.

3. They placed her, as beseemed a young and widowed princess, in the palaces of two ecclesiastics; Durham House in town, and Croydon Park among the Surrey Hills. A pile of ampler size and greater

splendour than the Priory of Clerkenwell, Durham House, the London palace of the bishop-palatine, rose on the water-edge adjoining Ivy Lane. A square, with inner court and flanking towers, the palace had a look of strength more seemly in a baron's castle than a bishop's house. Yet Durham House was a delicious seat. A noble garden lay around, ascending from the tide-way to the Strand. A stair and water-gate gave access to a fleet of boats. A lofty turret, springing from the front, commanded every ait and inlet of the stream from Lambeth spire to London Bridge. A prelate's house and garden lay to right and left; here Norwich Inn, there Carlisle Place; and southward, from the water stretched a green and wooded upland to the crest of Denmark Hill. This princely pile was empty; Fox, late Bishop of Durham, having gone to Winchester, and Lever, his successor in the see, being still the occupant of Carlisle Place. Thus, Durham House was free to Catharine; from whose tenancy it was to be a centre of historic scenes, which were to pass from Catharine of Aragon to Lady Jane Grey, from Lady Jane Grey to Princess Elizabeth, and from Princess Elizabeth to Sir Walter Raleigh. Catharine, with her maids, her servants, and her priests, took up her rest at Durham House.

4. The park at Croydon had been tenanted by archbishops from the Saxon times. All through the Norman reigns that park had been the country-seat of primates. Here Courtney had received his pall. Here Arundel and Chichele had lived. In Croydon, James the First, King of Scots, had been received

in his captivity. Here Morton had kept a splendid household. Deane was in possession; but the primate was at Lambeth, busy with affairs of state; and Catharine had the full enjoyment of his country-seat. The palace stood beside the church; a quaint old edifice, with guard-room, hall, and chapel; rich in carvings, shields, and royal arms. A verdant sward ran upward from this palace into planted clumps and breezy knolls. Whatever art could do to perfect nature had been done at Croydon Park. Archbishop Chichele had spent a fortune on the church and palace. All these beauties were her own; for Deane, a man of politics and business, had no time to spare for visiting his country-house. So busy was he with the King's affairs, that he had found no time to be enthroned, and was compelled to name a suffragan—John Bell—to do his duties in connexion with the Church. Thus, Catharine, though a guest in clerical houses, was entirely free from clerical invasion and control. Her ghostly needs were left in Padre Alessandro's charge.

5. At either Durham House or Croydon Park, the widow passed her early weeks of mourning with her chaplain, her dueña, and the ladies of her train. At first she lived in deep retirement, seeing no one save the King and Queen, the women of her chamber, and the tutor of her youth. The Queen, so good and true to all who were in grief, was more than good and true to Catharine in her lonely and uncertain state. The King was eager, not to say impatient. Day and night he asked himself if Henry, Duke of York, was now his heir? That stalwart boy

had been intended for the Church. His education had been settled with a view to clerical affairs; a bishop's staff, a cardinal's hat, and perhaps a papal crown. Were other things in store for him? Was he to live and die a secular prince? No one could tell him. He must wait and see.

6. The King was eager, with a passion not to be appeased. When business carried him away from town, a messenger brought him daily news from Croydon Park. His rivals were astir. Edmond de la Pole was working in the imperial court; and Henry was but poorly satisfied by having that rival burned in effigy at St. Paul's. While England had no Prince of Wales, there was no legal and accepted heir. Some persons held that if the reigning king should die, no prince could be proclaimed, no oath of fealty could be sworn, no legal process could be served, and everything would become the prey of chance. The risk was fearful; yet the council saw no way to bridge the chasm. They had to wait, and by their waiting prove, that Catharine was, in their belief, an actual widow of the Prince.

CHAPTER IV.

Estrada's Mission.

1502.

1. By the end of May, Estrada was in London; having ridden from Toledo, crossed the sea, and spurred from Dover to the Strand in less than twenty days. Such work as his brooked no delay. While he was on the road, he heard that Louis, King of France, was tempting Henry to his side by offering him a sister of Francois, Duke of Angoulême, for his son the Duke of York. The tale was true. Before he flung his troops across the Alps, that cautious prince was anxious to secure his capital from attack. All forms were studied and all means were tried to win a treaty of alliance from the English court. Francois was the King's cousin, and his sister, Madame Marguerite, was a lovely girl. If Louis were to leave no son behind him, Francois would be King of France. As yet he had no son. According to the policy laid down when he advised his cousin Charles to marry Duchess Anne, Louis, on coming to the throne, had sought the means of casting off his first wife, Jeanne de France, that he might take the royal widow and secure her duchy for the crown. As ready with his honours as his ducats, he had found a way of reconciling Rome.

The reigning pope was Alexander the Sixth, whose natural son, Cesare Borgia, had resigned his priesthood and his cardinal's hat. Amboise, who managed the affairs in Rome, had offered Alexander's son the duchy of Tarentum and the hand of Carlotta, Princess of Naples, as the price of a divorce. The Borgias had accepted his proposals. Amboise had been appointed judge, and Jeanne, a plain, weak woman, who had lived a blameless life for twenty years with Louis, had been cast aside. Amboise had been made a cardinal, and Louis had espoused the Duchess Anne. Yet no great blessing had accrued to them. No son had yet been born to wear the double crown, and Francois, Duke of Angoulême, was still the next of kin. A match between the Duke of York and Madame Marguerite was so wise and natural an arrangement, that Estrada feared it had already gone too far for him to spoil.

2. Estrada found the widowed girl at Durham House in perfect health. Nor was she suffering much in mind, excepting from the wrangles in her anteroom. Her household was in great disorder. No one would obey, and every one would rule. Puebla could not bear Elvira, and Elvira could not keep on terms with the ambassador. The chaplain, upright in his service, thwarted the dueña, who was pulling towards another point. Manrique quarrelled with Cuero and his wife. Since Arthur's death Sir Richard Pole had left the household, and Manrique and Cuero had resumed their posts as chamberlain and keeper of the plate. Like many of their betters, they forgot, on their return to power, the lesson of

their fall, and took to bickering in the closet on the day of their return.

3. Estrada lodged himself at Durham House with Catharine, where his rank and office gave him an authority with page and chamberlain beyond his formal warrants from the King and Queen. Sir Richard Croft and Bishop Smyth remained in Wales. Excepting William Holybrand, who spoke Castillian, not a man of English birth remained at Catharine's side. The ladies, too, were gone. No English person interfered; and yet her halls were loud with strife, Manrique thought he should be master everywhere, because he got his orders from the Princess, while Cuero thought he should be master in the jewel-room, because he got his orders from the King. "Regard the cups and jewels as your life; retain them under lock and key; refuse to lend them out for use; and see that none of them be either lost or sold"—such were Fernando's orders to his keeper of the plate. Cuero stood upon his duty; and the war of keeper, chamberlain, and dueña, was at issue when Estrada came and took upon himself the management of Catharine's house. His orders were to be discreet, and see that every one about him was discreet. The double object which he had in view required the nicest care, and he was forced to arm himself on every side. No matter what was said, he had to hold his tongue, though he might open eyes to every sight, and ears to every sound. He was to learn all facts and send reports of them to Spain, since facts would be the surest guide in every step they had to take.

4. Estrada told the Princess little; and he warned Elvira to be cautious in her speech. Too many things, he said, were blurted out. The King and Queen, their masters, wanted servants who had open ears and silent tongues. The maids of honour must be checked; and no one, either man or woman, must be suffered to exchange one word with Catharine on her future course of life. He, only, had a leave to speak. He only could employ another voice to speak. If it were known that Catharine had a female friend, that friend was never, under any pretext, to be left alone with her an instant. No one who enjoyed her confidence must see her, lest the question of her future should be raised. She was to hear no news, to form no plans, to dream no dreams. Estrada wished to see how far the field lay open to his arts before he let the Princess know what new articles he had in charge.

5. A seal being put on Catharine's maids, Estrada turned to her confessor. This Italian knew too much, and was too good a priest, he found, for what he had to do. He must be got away, and that before one word was said about a second match. As soon as Catharine knew what he was doing she was sure to tell the Padre, and the Padre might reply at once that such a thing could never be. Yet he was sent to Spain in such a guise that neither he nor Catharine guessed the reasons why he was recalled. Estrada told him that the King had need of him in State affairs; and when he placed the letter of recall in the confessor's hands, he urged him to depart at once for Spain. "You are to manage so that Ales-

sandro shall return," the King and Queen had written; "but you are not to let him see that you know anything of his note; consult with Doña Elvira; do what is best, and what seems good to her and you." Estrada put the priest on board a ship, and Catharine saw her early friend no more. He went to Spain, where much was made of him by King and Queen, who kept him in their service, and took charge of his preferment in the Church. He died a bishop. Thus, the only man in Catharine's house who could have given her sound advice, was snatched away from her before a word was whispered of this project for a second match.

6. A duke, a chamberlain, a privy-councillor, Estrada was received by Henry with the brightest smiles. They were beginning now to know him, even in Spain. But when the Duke, who rode to Windsor, spoke to Henry of his secret object, he observed a change of tone. The cause he had to plead was not an English cause, nor were the means by which he pressed that cause acceptable to the Tudor Prince. The English people were at peace; Estrada wished them to engage in war. The English ruler was allaying factious heats; Estrada wanted him to light the dying fires. By prudent steps the council was promoting unity of feeling through the land; Estrada bade them interrupt this noble labour by a roll of drums. Renouncing his imaginary rights in France, the King had fixed his mind on a pacific growth at home; Estrada urged him to renew an ancient and a fatal claim. Louis was paying to the English treasury fifty thousand crowns a-year;

Estrada would have had the King renounce this revenue. A great majority of the people hoped to see the Prince of Wales espouse a sister of the Duke of Angoulême; Estrada charged them to refuse all terms of friendship with the King of France. The special reasons for rejecting his proposals were as strong as the more general reasons. Since his coming to the throne, the King had studied, year by year, to purge his family of his original defects of title; and Estrada offered him a lady for his heir whose union would endanger the legitimacy of every future king. The council were in fear of Pole; Estrada was proposing an alliance that would give a host of partizans to the Yorkist prince. The English people were attached to law and order, to the rules of justice and the words of Holy Writ; Estrada tempted them to enter on a project that would bring them into conflict with the voice of Nature and the testament of God.

7. A man so close as Henry Tudor was not likely to betray his mind too soon. He had to hold his own with kings who played their game with loaded dice. Estrada's offers were a gain to him. They told him what the Queen of Spain desired. They warned him of a peril in his path. To send these offers to his council was to gain some months of time, and news might come at any hour from Italy that would dictate his future course. Great armies were approaching, and the echoes of their guns might soon be heard. Like other men, he was the slave of victory. Until Gonsalvo's guns could speak, the matter would be nicely left to councillors and judges,

who might find excuses for delay. Estrada soon became aware that he must meet objections to his offer raised by priests and jurists in the name of public law. Two parties showed themselves in council, each supposing that the King, though silent and reserved, was with them in his heart. Fox, Bishop of Winchester, was in favour of receiving the proposals sent from Spain; of studying them in detail, and resolving whether they were useful to the King and country. Warham, Bishop-elect of London, was in favour of rejecting them without discussion, as an outrage on his sovereign, on his country, and his God.

CHAPTER V.

Isabel's Orders.

1502.

1. From her apartments in Toledo, Isabel had to watch the progress of intrigue, in Paris, Rome, and Naples, and to guide her chamberlain in London by the light of many camps. Fernando had departed for the Aljaferia, where his presence was required among his troops. Louis was massing corps in Languedoc, and menacing her husband's duchies in the Pyrenees. In Rome, Cesare Borgia was at work with murderous knife, and still more murderous pen. Nemours, who had denounced the peace with Spain, was pressing on Gonsalvo. Louis himself was marching through the Alps. At home she was no less uneasy than abroad. Those Friends of Light, who hated her and her Inquisitors, were at work. She could not trust the councillors at her board, the doctors in her colleges, and the officers in her towns. In spite of her familiars, she was still regarded as a bigot and usurpress, who had sold her honesty for a crown. Alone in her high tower, the Queen was looking on these stormy skies, and having taken the affairs of Catharine into charge, she penned a letter to the Duke, at Durham House, in which she let him see her inmost soul. Her note

was couched in cyphers; two of her most secret cyphers. No man save the Duke was ever to have read this letter from the Queen of Spain.

2. "You are to understand," she wrote, "the King of France is on his way to Milan, and has sent an army against us with the design, it is said, of taking from us our estates. He has sent to the frontier of Perpignan many armed men, both foot and horse, and has commanded that ban and reban be proclaimed within his countries.... Thus, you see, how much we need to press. Let there be no delay in making an agreement for the contract of our daughter with the future Prince of Wales. This contract is the more necessary, as the King of France is seeking to prevent it; hoping to obtain the English alliance, and to get the Prince for either his daughter, or a sister of the Duke of Angoulême. Without saying a word about the last affair—since it is already known for a certainty that the Princess of Wales remains as she was when here—(for so Doña Elvira has written to us)—get the contract signed at once. Do not wait to consult with us. Delay is dangerous. See that the articles be written, signed and sworn. If nothing better can be got, let the affair be settled as we first proposed. In that case put it down in writing that the King of England has already received from us 100,000 scudos in gold. Let that payment be made a binding article with a view to restitution, in accordance with the order sent to you at first. Promise that we will pay the second part when the marriage shall have been completed; that is to say, if you shall not be able to obtain for

us more time. Take heed, that you on no account agree to pay what still remains of the dowry till the rite is over. See at once, moreover, that the King of England gives our daughter whatever money may be needed for her maintenance and that of her suite. Provide that in the arrangement of her household, everything shall be done to please the King of England. Take care that Doña Elvira shall remain with her, as well as any other person whom she may wish to keep."

3. Her Highness could not stay her pen. "Be very vigilant about this matter," she went on. "Do not let them see that you suspect anything; and do not show such eagerness as might induce the other side to cool. Set about our business prudently, and in the manner which may seem best to you, so that no delay may happen. Let us know what you have done. You must not wait for our advice. You know our will." The passion of her pleading droops at last into a worldly tone. "A league of amity," she adds, "was long ago concluded between us and the King of England, binding us to aid each other in defending our estates. That treaty says, *in what we possess at present*, that is to say, what we possessed when the treaty was made. According to that treaty, therefore, England is not obliged to aid us in defending Apulia and Calabria, because we have obtained those countries since the draft was signed. When the treaty of marriage is made, you shall say to the King of England that it is reasonable, since the treaty of kinship is being settled afresh, he should renew the treaty of amity in such a manner that,

without altering anything except the date, all that we have mentioned may be done. The former articles are clear in this respect; if you think well, make use of them; but you must get the articles signed at once."

4. Nothing could have been better for the Spanish queen, nothing could have been worse for the English people, than a mere renewal of the articles of peace. To guarantee her holding of Granada was a daring step; for many fierce revolts, and some amazing victories, had shown how strong the Moorish feeling was; and Spain was so afraid of interference, that the Queen had sent her scribe, Pietro Martire, to appease the Soldan. Henry had guaranteed that conquest of the Cross. But the Italian provinces of Spain were even less secure. A host of rivals claimed them; Louis of France, Alexander the Sixth, Federigo the First, Cesare Borgia. Spain had sought adventures on Italian soil; at one time with the French against the Pope, another time with the Pope against the French; and now she was at war with both the spiritual pastor and the temporal prince. For England to adopt a guarantee of what she held by force in Naples was to clothe herself with troubles which could yield no glory, and might cost much coin and blood. It was to undertake a permanent war against the French. Estrada was requested by his Queen to treat this article as a thing of form; and be extremely guarded in his speech on French affairs. The English King was not to guess how matters stood with them in France; and only after he had signed a treaty, binding Spain

and England to assist each other in their wars, was he to learn that Louis and Fernando had already drawn the sword.

5. "Before you speak one word to the King of England about the King of France," she said, "we want the marriage to be settled, so that fear of war may not prevent the match. On this account, it would be well that you should do things quickly. If anything is said to you about a war with France, pretend you do not believe it. Say so till the treaty of marriage has been signed. When that is done, you must show the King of England the Relation, which we send you herewith, of the matters between us and the King of France." Not sure that Henry was so ill informed about her dealings with the court of France, she added, as a postscript: "If, by chance, the rupture between the King of France and ourselves should be already known in England, and there should seem to be any disposition on the part of Henry to recover Guienne and Normandie by uniting himself with us, and us with him, in that case, let him understand that Max, the Emperor, will be on our side. In fact, should you find that your negotiation will be easier, and the state of our affairs with France shall render it necessary, try to get the King of England to engage in war, by telling him that he will never have another such chance of recovering his lost domains. We think it would be well to make use of Doctor De Puebla in these negotiations. If you think he will be of use to you, explain the business to him, and let him give you aid in any way that seems the

best. Try to persuade the King of England to engage in this affair. Use all the skill that we expect from you, and give it all your time and thought. If anything be said to you by others, listen; negotiate with caution; and consult with us should need arise. You must not say one word, however, till you have been certified of our actual rupture with the French."

6. By Isabel's own showing then, this union of Catharine with her brother-in-law, the Duke of York, though known to be illegal, was contrived by her in order that, by means of English landings on the coast of France, she and the King, her husband, might be able to retain the provinces they had seized in Italy from the lawful prince. It was the counterpart of what she had already done in Lisbon. To attain this worldly end, she felt no scruple in cajoling and deceiving every one in turn—her priest, her ally, and her child.

CHAPTER VI.

A Spanish Comedy.

1502.

1. Before Estrada could report his doings, Isabel, in her lonely house, impatient for success, gave eye and ear to Puebla, and began to waver in her plan of trusting to the Duke. The doctor was in bitter mood. This fool of quality who had come to London was a greater insult to his pride than the urbane and able priest. Estrada treated him with cold and lofty airs. To find out what the Duke had come to do, and when he knew the business, to defeat it, had been Puebla's first resolves on finding the grandee at Durham House. A priest like Puebla, known to every councillor, and free from every scruple, had the means of thwarting such an enemy as the Duke. He warned his mistress that the Duke would fail. Much personal tact, much knowledge of the world, he told her, were essential to success in London; but the envoy she had sent to carry out her will had neither personal tact nor knowledge of the world. If she desired to gain her ends, she must employ her old and faithful servant. He, who knew the ground, could tread it with a certain foot. A stranger to the country could not help but fail. If she would deign to

trust him and employ him, he would soon create that "new world" in her affairs of which he had written to her so many times. She read his words, and half relented of her harshness towards the man. Already she had been compelled to seek his help. When Isabel learnt that her proposals had been met by legal queries which Estrada could not answer, she had told the Duke to call in Puebla, if he thought the doctor honest, and the Duke, without pretending to believe him honest, had been forced to call him in. In treating with a man like Warham, no less sharp in law than subtle in the use of words, Estrada was completely lost, and Puebla saw with glee that the most difficult part of the affair was falling day by day into his hands.

2. He won the Queen of Spain by sending her a piece of secret news. The English King, he said, admitted that the royal widow was entitled to receive her rents; a sum of twenty-five thousand crowns of gold a-year. The same admission had, he said, been made by Savage, once commissioner at Medina, now Archbishop of York. Such news was welcome at Toledo. Puebla added, for himself, that he had always said the King of England must restore the hundred thousand crowns; and he presumed to send to her the details of a plan for bringing both the King and council to her feet. She liked his view, and liked his plan. As ready to employ as to condemn a servant, Isabel took the doctor to her heart and held her dark familiars in reserve. She even stooped to coax the cripple; begging him to forget her former slights; and pro-

mising him the highest favour if he should persuade the council to adopt her views. It was no light affair, she wrote, nor would his recompense be small. "If there is any service man could do for me, here is that service to be done." She bade him act for her as he saw good, and take advantage of the Duke being near him. Puebla, when he got this letter, was elate with joy.

3. In all the comic writing of her country there is nothing droller than the letter Isabel addressed that evening to Estrada. She was still alone. Fernando could not leave the Aljaferia, where a thousand public cares engrossed his mind. French corps were forming in his front, with a design of rushing at the Pyrenees. A dangerous spirit was abroad in many of his towns, where few, except the lowest rabble, could endure his consort's Acts of Faith. In Italy, Nemours had driven Gonsalvo from the field; and he was doubting whether Spain could keep a footing in the towns. The French had suddenly displayed a vast array of force. Gonsalvo had to seek for safety in Barletta, an obscure and ill-protected harbour on the eastern coast, where he was forced to wait for men and guns, exposed to insults from an enemy whose military talents he despised. The Pope had formed a close alliance with Louis, who had made his son a duke, and married him to a sister of Jean, king-consort of Navarre. Cesare Borgia, having quitted Rome for Lombardy, was welcoming Louis on Italian ground. At Milan, which the King of France had entered as a conqueror, Cesare was received with joy. As Venice

was engaged in war with Bajazet, all Italy appeared to lie at Louis' feet.

4. The Queen took up her pen and wrote (in substance) to Estrada: "It is now too late. Affairs are so much worse, that if we ask for a betrothal we shall be refused. Even if the King of England hears of what is done, we shall be greatly hurt. Press, therefore, for my daughter's quick return to Spain. She can display her grief far more at home than she can do in England, where the custom of the country is against display of grief. Tell Henry that we cannot bear to have a daughter whom we love so far away from home. A girl of Catharine's age is better in her mother's house. Request his leave to bring her home. Let some one of a proper age be named to come with her and see her safely landed on our shores." These words were all a comedy. No part of her instructions was to be adopted, save in show and with a purpose to deceive. Instead of wanting Catharine nearer home, the Queen was bent on marrying her to the English heir. The plan had many details. "Tell his Highness that you have instructions to engage a fleet of ships." In order to deceive the King a show of active preparation must be made. The household must be thoroughly misled. "You are to lay commands on every one. A captain will arrive in London. See him, and arrange the cost of freight with him. He must be made to think you are about to sail. Allow some members of the train to go on board."

5. Thus far the thing was easy, but the Queen

went on to overdo her part. Estrada was to speak as though the going of the Princess meant a restitution of her hundred thousand crowns. He was to let the King and councillors understand that he expected every scudo of that money to be put on board his ships. The law had said it was her right. That law must be obeyed; but even if it were not law, so wise and good a prince as Henry could not suffer Catharine, in her dreadful sorrow, to be stript of everything she had. If Henry pointed to the marriage articles, Estrada must request him to point out any article in the treaty of alliance which said he was *not* to return the money. If Henry feigned that he knew nothing of Spanish law, Estrada was to answer that the Queen knew nothing of English law. If Henry said he was not bound to pay by law, he must be asked to pay because he ought to pay. How could he think of robbing a young lady who had suffered so much misery in his kingdom? Enemies and infidels could do no worse. "You are to ask and to insist on having Catharine given into your charge, together with her plate and jewels, and her hundred thousand crowns."

6. Estrada carried out her orders so that every one at Durham House and Croydon Park believed he was about to sail. Manrique got the household ready to embark. Esquivel tried to square accounts. Cuero packed his plate and jewels, and arranged for carrying them on board. A ship lay waiting in the Thames. The skipper came to Durham House; some members of the household went on board his ship. A troop of swarthy seamen

loitered round the stairs, and every idler near the water-side could see that active preparations were afoot. Ayala was already gone. Estrada was about to go with Catharine. Puebla was unlikely to remain. The Duke, however, kept a prudent course. His orders were precise, and he was not to go beyond the line laid out. "The only object of these measures," Isabel had told him, "is to bring the business of betrothal to a close. Let this be done as fast as you can force it on. Let it be done as we desire. When that is done, our cares will cease. Then we can ask for English help against the French. No other arm can aid us in our strait." She closed with a pathetic hint. "It is for me," she said, "that you have now to strive. I look for you to do your utmost. If you ever hope to serve me, you must do it now. The service to be done for us in England is the greatest in the world."

CHAPTER VII.

A Change of Front.

1502.

1. BEFORE she knew the issue of her plan, the Queen, more anxious every hour, had formed another scheme. A fresh ambassador should go to Henry's court. The King, her lord, was no less fretful than herself. Gonsalvo was constrained to act on the defensive. Rome had turned against him. Alexander the Sixth had cast his lot with France, intending, with the help of Louis, to bequeath a family kingdom, with a temporal capital in Rome. The Pope had given his daughter, Lucrezia, poisoner and murderess, in marriage to Alfonzo d'Este. Cesare Borgia, armed by France, was ravaging Bologna and Perugia. Florence was not safe from the rapacious duke. On every side the French were present in amazing force. A fleet and army lay at Genoa, ready to descend on any point. A corps of Swiss and Gascons were proceeding through a friendly country towards the south. Their aim was Naples. Sicily was menaced from the sea, and little had been done to meet an enemy attacking from the north. Louis was in Milan, acting like a King of Italy; receiving embassies, rewarding princes, lecturing common-

wealths, and raising troops and money for his war. No terms that Spain could offer were acceptable to Louis. With a lofty manner he received Fernando's agents, and dismissed them with a loud and scornful speech. "Retire," he said in substance, "from the Capitanata; otherwise, I will take Apulia and Calabria from you."

2. Spain was ill prepared for war. The country was uneasy, and Fernando feared to send his troops abroad. Granada was excited by a hope of foreign troubles, which might draw the garrisons of Loja, Gaudix, and Alhama, towards the Pyrenees. Fierce risings, fiercely quelled, had kept the bitter blood alive in every glen of Andalus where a Mohammedan people held the soil. At any moment they might rise again. Two years ago, the Moorish battle of Monarda had excited every capital in Europe. Even Asia heard the yell of victory. When Martire reached the Nile, on his pacific mission to the Soldan, he was warned to re-embark at once; the passions of the people being so hot against his master that the Soldan's officers would not answer for his head. Martire's quick Italian brain suggested that this peril, whether great or little, must be braved. If he retired, a fleet might follow in his wake. He sailed for Cairo, saw the Soldan, and with soft Italian wiles appeased the anger of that mighty prince. But no one knew how long his patience would endure, and if he chose to send a fleet to Malaga while Spain was closing in a hug of life and death with France, the gains of twenty years might all be lost. Nor was

Fernando safer in the north than in the south. The Catalans were enraged against his Holy Office, and this rage extended through the Pyrenees. This feeling opened many a door for the intrigues of France. In letters and theology, the French were liberal, and the brightness of their wit, no less than the vivacity of their lives, gave wing and vogue to what they said. The Catalans were strong in national feeling, but their sense of unity had been wasting in those fierce inquisitorial fires. With every year the French got closer to the Pyrenees. Navarre was still unfriendly. Alain d'Albret, father of the King, was getting ready to conduct an army, by the road of Irun, into Spain. Descending from Pamplona, he could swoop on either Zaragoza or Valladolid, in either of which capitals a liberal soldier, preaching French ideas in theology and government, might find a host of friends.

3. Guter Gomez de Fuensalida, one of the ablest servants in her court, was going to Flanders on the Archduke's business. Isabel bade him pass by way of London, where he was to see and help the Duke. Don Guter was in all her secrets; knowing the objects of her policy, and the means through which she hoped to gain her ends. To him she spoke of things she hardly cared to write; for what is writ remains in evidence, and what she had to say was not the stuff that people write on tombs. "Give heed to what Don Guter says," she wrote to Puebla. "He can tell you what we want," she warned Estrada, "not in what concerns the treaty and betrothal merely, but in what con-

cerns the help we need from England in our wars." Fernando, who was seeking allies even in the homes of counts and cardinals, was hot for English help, as being the only help that was of instant use. For what great prize, he asked, would England go to war? Would she be tempted by an offer of Guienne and Normandie? If so, the King of Spain would help her with his utmost power in wresting those great provinces from the French. Fernando was prepared to yield his right of making peace. Should Henry doubt him still, he was prepared to give securities for his good faith. But every point, he urged, should be arranged at once, in order that an English army might be hurled at France.

4. While Guter tarried by the road, a batch of letters reached Madrid, a hunting lodge to which the King and Queen had come to spend their Christmas-tide. These letters, written by Estrada, put another aspect on affairs. They told her Grace, that things were better at the English court; that Henry's council was divided in opinion; that a draft of articles had been drawn by friends of Spain; and that the King himself, though silent and inscrutable, was secretly in favour of the match. If all these things were so, the game was in their hands. They wrote to tell Estrada that he need not wait Don Guter's coming. He might even order Puebla home; entrapping him on board a ship by promises that he should soon go back. No one must interrupt a labour which had taken this auspicious turn.

5. Under this new idea that the King of England wished his son to marry Catharine, Isabel told the Duke, her envoy, what he ought to say and do. He must be cold in word and slow in deed. He was to treat with Henry as the wooer, not the wooed, and lead the world in general to infer that Windsor was soliciting a favour at Madrid. He was to drop all question of Guienne and Normandie, and think of nothing but the marriage. Other things would come in time. But more than all, Estrada was to let the King of England understand that Isabel was conscious of his wishes in the matter, and was giving him the highest proof of her regard in listening to the offers he was pressing on her husband and herself!

6. She had begun to fear the odium that must cling to those who were supposed to have imagined such a marriage. Alessandro had returned; she could not well avoid some talk with him on Catharine's life in Ludlow; and from habit she had always listened to his honest voice. She told her envoy that the odium of originating this alliance must be cast on England. Even in the treaty, Henry must be represented as the one who had been first to move, and Isabel as the last who had been brought to yield. Henry must be induced, not only to accept of Catharine for his son, but to demand her with such haste and passion, that if shame should come of the affair, that shame would fall on him and not on her. In this new mood of mind, she bade the Duke take note that nothing would be done by him unless he put the treaty into such a

shape as would leave her blameless in the eyes of men. She pointed out the way in which she wished this story of her offer to be read; for she was always dreaming of the after time; and thinking how the world would speak of her when she was dead. She meant the tale to run, that Henry and Elizabeth, in order to promote the welfare of their states, had urged her to allow their son, the Duke of York, to marry Catharine; and that she, a good and pious Queen, had met these English overtures with great reserve. She meant it to be told that Henry, acting through his council, had implored her to consent; and that, in pity for their misery, and on grounds of public policy, she had been induced to sacrifice herself. "You are to go at once to the King," she wrote, "and speak to him about the betrothal of our daughter with the Prince. In doing so, you shall tell him we are well aware how much he seeks to bring this match about. And you shall tell him that on account of the love we bear him, and the good we see in it for every one, we have agreed to grant his prayer." Estrada was to drop one further hint. "You are to let his highness understand that we are pleased to see this match take place, because it is good for him and for his realm to be assured of our friendship, and also that of our children and our people, just as it may be good for us to have his friendship now, and in the time to come."

BOOK THE NINTH.

THE ENGLISH COURT.

CHAPTER I.

King and Queen.

1502-3.

1. THE year of mourning for their son was spent by Henry and Elizabeth in deeper privacy than ever. Arthur was gone from them; their child, their perfect knight, their prince of song and legend, was no more. Camelot was now a silent city, and Pendragon slept beside that tomb in Worcester where the tapers burnt and mass was sung in honour of the dead. Would Heaven renew to them that loss? Old men who read the stars assured them that the coming year would bring them happier days. That coming year, these sages said, would prove a crown and solace to the Queen. What love could ask and art devise, in memory of the Prince, was done by them. His tomb was treated as a shrine. His will was faithfully observed. His widow was adopted as a daughter of the royal house. The palaces in which his youth had passed

became the objects of their melancholy choice. At every stage of his career religion had been made a witness and a partner of his course. A lady chapel had been built in Winchester where he was born; a chantry had been raised at Farnham, whither he was sent to nurse. Sheen, Eltham, Greenwich, all his favourite homes, had cells without, and shrines within, their gates. These cells and chapels were the objects of their love.

2. If public cares disturbed the King, he tried to shut them out. He soothed the anguish of his soul with secret hope, and with the works of piety and mercy which alone could bring him peace. The day on which the King and Queen were stricken down, on which their hearts were drawn so closely to each other, seemed to lengthen out into a second bridal year. At length, as autumn came, the Queen could whisper words to flood his anxious eyes with light.

3. One duty of these days of mourning was the building of a chapel near the palace gates in which they hoped to slumber side by side, when they had won their rest. At first, this pile had been projected as a shrine; the temple of a royal saint; but though St. Henry had become a popular idol, he had not, as yet, been canonised in Rome. The shrine was turned into a sepulchre and chapel of a line of Tudor kings. The Saxon transept and the Norman aisles were full. Between the ashes of St. Edward, Henry of Azincour, and Edward the Black Prince, no space was left for royal tombs. When Lady Elizabeth died, it had been hard to

find a spot in which to lay their child. If Tudor princes were to rest beneath that minster roof, another chapel must be built. Already Henry had prepared a tomb in Windsor, but a wider sweep of thought induced him to abandon that design.

4. His consort had a liking for the abbey. Next to John the Evangelist, St. Peter was her chosen saint; the cloister was her favourite walk; the abbot, Islip, was her personal friend. In early days the Queen had found a refuge with the monks; in later times, the artist who had since become an abbot, had adorned her service-book. More public reasons swayed the King. No edifice in his country could pretend to vie with the great minster as a monument of kings, and as a witness and memorial of events. Sebert, King of the East Saxons, had erected the original church, as evidence of his conversion to the cross. Edgar, King of England, aided by St. Dunstan, had rebuilt that church, in memory of the close of a dynastic war. Edward the Confessor, after pulling down the older piles, had raised a temple worthy of St. Peter, as a nation's thanks to God for her return to independent rule. Henry the Third and Edward the First had beautified the church, in which was placed the sacred rock of Scone; a witness that the kingdoms of the north and south had been united to the farthest isles. All changes in the nation's course had been recorded in this abbey church. Here slept the holiest Saxon prince and mightiest Saxon saint. Beneath this roof a Norman Duke had been anointed King, and here, in every age, his followers had been crowned.

5. Another day of change had come; a day of change as great as any that had happened in preceding times. A civil war had closed in peace. A union of the rival lines had been secured, and faction had been almost crushed. Wales, so long estranged from her great neighbour, had been reconciled in the presence of a prince of Cymric blood. An English government had been planted in the Irish soil. A prospect had been opened for a second and pacific union of the south and north. Nay, changes more profound were taking place around him; for the age of feudal violence was passing out of sight, and life and thought were taking more domestic and poetic forms. So vast a change should leave a record on the minster, and the King was moved to write that record in his noblest style. A chapel rich and rare should rise against the abbey and become a part of it. Sir Reginald Bray and Abbot Islip were employed in laying out the plans, and in their year of mourning Abbot Islip laid the first stone of the magnificent pile in which the royal mourners had agreed to sleep their silent sleep.

CHAPTER II.

Works of Mercy.

1502-3.

1. IN spite of what old men who read the stars had promised her, the Queen was anxious. Offerings to the saints were multiplied. A priest went up and down the land, to Worcester, Ipswich, Woodstock, and Northampton, to deposit alms and offer prayers in her behalf. St. George was much besought. St. Henry was not forgotten. Every shrine that a Madonna was supposed to favour was adorned with gifts. Our Lady of Eton and our Lady of Caversham were besought. The Holy Cross at Windsor, and the Child of Grace at Reading, were implored for aid. The Queen herself set out on pilgrimage. Shrine after shrine was sought, and every day her journey through the land was marked by gentle deeds; by feeding the poor, clothing the naked, helping the infirm.

2. While the anxious Queen was out on pilgrimage, the King was busy with improvements in his capital. The priory of St. John of Clerkenwell was much enlarged. Baynard Castle was completed as a personal residence for the Queen. An abbot's house was being built in Westminster. All these additions to his capital were built in that domestic

and pacific style which marked the close of an old reign of strife, when every man's house was his castle, and every man's life depended on his coat of mail. One type of what this reign of peace was calling into being, was a project for converting the great palace of Savoy into a hospital for the poor.

3. This pile was dear to Henry as a special heritage of the house of Lancaster. Built by Peter of Savoy, Earl of Richmond, it had come to Edward, first Earl of Lancaster, by whom it had been greatly strengthened and enlarged. Thus early had the names of Lancaster and Richmond been united. Once again these names of Lancaster and Richmond had been wedded at the Savoy, when Blanche, sole daughter of Henry, first Duke of Lancaster, had married John of Gaunt, twelfth Earl of Richmond, who had afterwards been created second Duke of Lancaster. Henry the Fourth had made the Savoy a second Tower. Too vast for any subject to reside in, it was left in lonely splendour by the Thames, except when some great sovereign had to be received in state. Here John of France had lived and died. In common speech, the Savoy was regarded as the house of John of Gaunt. Wat Tyler had destroyed it out of spite for John of Gaunt; Jack Cade had ruined it a second time in spite for John of Gaunt. As Henry gazed upon the wide and ghastly wreck —fit emblem of a reign of feudal power, assailed and broken in a storm of popular wrath—a great conception came into his mind. This waste, he said, should be repaired. This site, so cursed to the old line of Lancaster, should be redeemed to

the new line of Lancaster. As yet, the Savoy was connected in the popular mind with deeds of violence; henceforth it should be known by acts of charity and peace.

4. Provision for the poor and sick was scanty, even in London, where the monks had priories and hospitals fit for princes of the blood. The dole served out at convent gates was meagre, and the shelter given in convent yards was rough. A poor man had no right within the convent walls, and in his wayside songs he raised his wail and curse. He saw a lordly pile of stone; he heard a glorious anthem in the church; he fancied a refectory warm with game and wine; and turned away from all this art and wealth, to munch in bitterness of heart his crust of barley bread. The monks had palaces like the priory of St. John, the priory of St. Bartholomew, the convent of Christ Church, the convent of the Crutched Friars; and yet those holy fathers had not built one fit receptacle for the blind and lame, the broken and insane. A hideous and contagious malady had caused the foundation of lazar-houses at St. James' in the Fields, St. Giles' in the Fields, St. Mary's in Kingsland, and in old Kent Road, where male and female lepers were received in fear and left to herd apart from men. These wretches were supposed to be accursed of God. Each lazar-house was parted from the nearest street by open fields, which the afflicted ones were not allowed to pass. If any one escaped, he was pursued with sticks and stones, and driven with imprecations to his lair. These lazar-houses were not

large, nor were the inmates many. Next to the lazar of St. James's, that of St. Mary, Kingsland, had the greatest name; yet Pope, a wealthy citizen, had bequeathed to it in sober charity a gift of eighty pence a year.

5. Four houses, if not more, called hospitals, existed in his capital; poor types of what was needed on the largest scale; St. Catharine's hospital near the Tower; St. Bartholomew's hospital near Smithfield; Elsinge's hospital near London Wall; and Bethlehem hospital near Bishop's Gate. All four were lay in origin and spirit. St. Catharine's hospital had been founded by the two Queens, Maud and Elinor, as a home for women. St. Bartholomew's hospital had been founded by the court jester, Rayer, for the treatment of disease. Elsinge's hospital had been built by William Elsinge, mercer, as an asylum for the blind. Bethlehem hospital had been endowed by Simon Fitzwary, sheriff, as a refuge for the hopelessly insane. These hospitals were small in size, and if the revenues of some were growing great, the money was consumed in buying plate and vestments rather than in building wards. A home for ten or twelve persons was esteemed a great affair. In every case the clerical staff was larger than the number of patients. For a dozen poor men or women there were twenty canons, priests, monks, nuns, and singing men. St. Catharine's hospital, near the Tower, was rich in silver cups, in jewelled crosses, in embroidered altar-cloths, but it was poor and weak at every point in which a public hospital should be strong. The wards were

few, the bread given out was scant; but in revenge the chapel was a gem of art, the garden worthy of a royal duke. St. Catharine's hospital was a palace of abuse.

6. Another sort of hospital was already taking shape in Henry's mind. It was to be connected with the memory of his son, for every gracious thought and pious deed were now connected with the memory of his peerless prince. A true asylum for the poor and helpless, with provision for a hundred beds at once, and means to add a second hundred beds soon after, was the royal dream. A chapel should be part of his foundation, with a modest service of Observant friars. This hospital should bear the name of John the Baptist, and a daily mass should be devoted in the chapel to the good of Arthur's soul. Clean beds and wholesome food must be provided. Every one should enter and retire at will. The doors were to be open, and the wards were to be free. In brief, his palace of the Savoy should be made a palace for the poor.

CHAPTER III.

Elizabeth the Good.

1503.

1. News came in from Italy, where a combat had been fought, which caused more stir in street and camp than many a field where crowns are lost and won. A knight, in heavy French array, was sneering at the lighter horse of Spain, attired and drilled in Moorish fashion. An indignant horseman answered that the Spanish cavalry were equal to the French. A combat was proposed; eleven selected knights being chosen to contend for victory on either side. A field was lent by a Venetian admiral at Trani, on the Adriatic coast, below the walls of that small harbour of Barletta in which Gonsalvo, closely, pressed by Nemours, was awaiting help from Spain. The bravest knights and swiftest riders were to lead the rest; Paredes on the Spanish side, and Bayard on the Gallic side. This fight came off, and lasted from the opening of the lists till dark. A blare of horns—a rush of steeds—a cry of *Vive la France!* —an answering cry of *Viva España!*—and a mass of mail and men lay sprawling on the ground. Four French steeds were dead. Three Spaniards were dismounted by the shock, but not one Spanish charger had been hurt. Again the horns gave

tongue; again the knights advanced. More horses fell. They fought all day with varying fortune. As the sun went down, the Venetian judges closed the lists. Two Frenchmen only, Bayard and another, had contrived to keep their seats. Seven Spaniards sat their saddles when the names were called. A Caliph might have bonneted to these Spanish knights; but neither side could claim a victory, since neither side had wholly cleared the ring.

2. This combat was the war in brief; and Henry had to wait, like the Venetian judges, for events to speak. If Nemours crushed Gonsalvo, Spain would be too much reduced to urge her project; if Gonsalvo routed Nemours and recovered Naples, she might press her project to the point of war. He knew the Queen of Spain, and he had no desire to fight. In truth, he wished Queen Isabel to regard him as her nearest ally, for he had an object to attain by her and through her of the highest moment, which he could not hope to gain against her will.

3. When he had met the Archduke Philip in a church near Calais, he had sounded him on certain schemes, and found the Archduke well content to meet his views. The Archduke's infant, Carl, was three months old, and Mary, Henry's youngest daughter, four years and three months old. He thought the boy and girl would make a pair, and he was sure that such a marriage would support the glory of his house. For Carl was heir of Germany and Spain; his wife would hold the highest female dignity on earth. But there were many ob-

stacles for him to overcome. The Emperor was unfriendly to his suit, and Philip, though he called him father, and professed to love him as a son, was playing an ambiguous game. Though talking to the King of Lady Mary, he was bargaining with Louis for the hand of Madame Claude. But Isabel was a greater obstacle than either Philip, Max, or Claude. Prince Carl was Isabel's next male heir, and her consent, with that of her estates, would have to be procured before the Prince could pledge himself to marry any one. That Isabel would start objections was a thing of course; that she would make conditions was a thing of course. If Henry meant to gain a hearing for his suit in Spain, he must be careful not to wake a sense of personal injury in Isabel's heart.

4. While every one was waiting on events, a change occurred at court which robbed the Princess Catharine of her truest friend. In spite of pious prayers and gentle deeds, the Queen continued frail in health. Her spirits sank within her as that hour approached of which she had been whispering to the King. A train of nurses came to Baynard Castle, where she loved to lodge, as having been her son's last home in London. An apartment in the Tower was put in order to receive her, for the King desired his second Arthur to be born in that old palace of his race. But he would not allow her to retire too soon. To cheer her mind, he carried her from house to house; rode down with her to Eltham, where the children had been nursed; held water parties for her on the Thames; and made a

merry Christmas-tide for her at Richmond Park. She entered into all his pastimes; played a game at cards; drank posset; chatted with Patch, her fool; looked on a Spanish dance; and listened while her minstrels sang. For each she had a smile and a reward. From Richmond stairs she rowed to Hampton Court, a favourite house with her; and strewing every path with gifts and graces dropt again to London, where at length she "took her room." Stern rules forbade the King to be with her; but he was nigh at hand in case his presence was desired. When she had passed into her rooms, the curtains closed on her, and she was lost to sight. A joiner put up shelves for books, and Patch took in a dish of pomegranates. On Candlemas-day her child was born; a girl, a lovely girl, yet one more helpless child, who brought no strength to her uncertain line. She heard the news, and never raised her head again. The stars had played her false; the King, her husband, had received a blow. She looked upon her infant's face; and called it by the name of that poor Lady of the Pomegranate, who, in circumstances strangely like, had caused her parents such a pang at Alcala. The Queen could do no more. Her strength was gone. Nine days she waited for the angels to descend. Her birthday came; her thirty-seventh year was done; and on that happy day she closed her eyes. The stars that promised her a crown had kept their word.

5. At first, the King could hardly think of peril in connexion with his wife. So young, so beautiful, so brave, what traffic could she have with death?

He sent for doctors far and near. One man of name, who lived near Gravesend, was compelled by him to travel through the wintry night, with guides and torches, from his village to the Tower. But whether he could see the thing or not, her time had come and gone. When all was over he retired into his room, nor would he suffer any one to break upon his lonely grief. The silent hours were long, and when he issued from his chamber to attend the council, it was noted that his eyes sought out the persons who had been about his wife. They needed much support, these faithful servants, for a sweeter mistress was not likely to be found again on earth. The King went up into their rooms, and sat with them, and spoke a word of comfort in their ears. Nor was he satisfied with speaking to the lords and ladies who had served her; for he sent Sir Charles Somerset and Sir Richard Guildford to every one, high and low, with his "good words" in dear remembrance of his wife. All pious pomp of woe was lavished on the partner of his youth. A grave was opened in that chapel near the Abbey church. The infant, too, had fallen asleep and was no more. Mother and child were laid together in the yet unfinished shrine; and underneath her chosen motto,

Humble and Penitent,

the earth was piled on all that men could see of what had been Elizabeth the Good.

NOTES AND DOCUMENTS.

FIFTH BOOK.
(Continued.)

CHAP. III.—1. Carvajal, *Documentos Ineditos*, XVIII. 278-281; Gayangos, *Moh. Dyn. Sp.* II. 390-392.

2. Passport for Antonio Geraldino (Arch. Gen. de la Cor. Aragon), Registros, 3549, f. 97; *Biog. Univ.* XVII. 165.

3. Bernaldes, *Reyes Catolicos*, c. 93.

4. My Note Book; Jones, *Palace of the Alhambra*, various plates; Gayangos, *Moh. Dyn. Sp.* I. 43, 44, II. 368.

5. Madoz, *Diccionario de España*, VIII. 468; Mariana, *Historia de España*, II. 511.

6. Puebla to Fernando and Isabel, July 17, 1498; Quintanillo, *Archetypo*, lib. II. c. 9; Fray Andreas to Juana, Sep. 1. 1498.

CHAP. IV.—1. Carvajal, *Documentos Ineditos*, XVIII. 282-4.

2. Richard, Duke of York, to Isabel, Sep. 8, 1493.

3. *Documents relating to Perkin Warbeck*, by Sir F. Madden; *Archaologia*, XXVII. 153; Gairdner, *Mem. Hen. Sev.* Pref. XXX. XXXVI.; Gairdner, *Letters and Papers*, II. L.-LX.; Bacon, *History of Henry the Seventh*, *Works*, VI. 132.

4. Fernando and Isabel to Puebla, April 14, 1496.

5. Bacon, *Works*, VI. 133-6.

6. Patent Rolls, Feb. 19, 1486, Feb. 26, 1488.

7. Bergenroth, *Cal. Span. Pap.* I. LXXXV.
8. Fernando and Isabel to Puebla, July 20, 1495.

CHAP. V.—1. Duchess Margaret to Alexander VI., in *Mem. Hen. Sev.* Ap. A. 323-9; Smith, *History of Cork*, I. 422.
2. Puebla to Fernando and Isabel, Aug. 25, 1498; *Calendar of the Carew MSS. preserved in the Archiepiscopal Library at Lambeth*, edited by J. S. Brewer and William Bullen (London, 1871), 472; *History of the Viceroys of Ireland*, by J. T. Gilbert (Dublin, 1865), 444; Gairdner, *Letters and Papers*, II. XLIX-LIII.
3. Bishop of Brixen to the Signory, May 5, June 14, July 11, 17, 1495; Contarini and Trevisano to the Signory, July 17, 1495; Brewer and Bullen, *Cal. Carew MSS.* 188.
4. Contarini to the Signory, May 1, June 9, 14, July 17, 1496; Ap. *Mem. Hen. Sev.* 393-9; *Pat. Rolls*, March 22, July 26, 1495.
5. *Collections for a History of Sandwich, in Kent*, by William Boys (Canterbury, 1792), 680; André, *Vit. Hen. Sep.* 69.
6. *Patent Rolls*, June 16, Sept. 21, 1494, July 26, 1495; *The Annals of Ireland*, translated from the original Irish of the Four Masters by Owen Connellan (Dublin, 1846), 319, 330.
7. *The Earls of Kildare and their Ancestors*, by the Marquis of Kildare, (Dublin, 1858), I. 47, 52, 56; Gilbert, *Viceroys of Ireland*, 448-56; Hook, *Archbishops of Canterbury*, V. 507-8; Brewer and Bullen, *Calendar of Carew MSS.* 179.
8. Contarini to the Signory, July 25, Aug. 16, 1495; Ryland, *History of Waterford*, 30, 31; Gilbert, *Viceroys of Ireland*, 457; Brewer and Bullen, *Cal. Car. MSS.* 472.

CHAP. VI.—1. Contarini and Trevisano to the Signory, Aug. 16, Dec. 10, 1495; Contarini to the Signory, Jan. 4, 6, 1496.
2. Fernando and Isabel to Puebla, Jan. 20, 1496; Guicciardini, *Storia d'Italia*, lib. II. c. III.; Sismondi, *Républiques Italiennes*, VI. 262-374; Bergenroth, *Cal. Span.*

Papers, I. art. 22; Ballaguer, *Historia de Cataluña*, lib. VIII. c. 31; New Treaty of Spain and England, Mar. 8, 1493; Puebla to Fernando and Isabel, Sep. 25, 1498.

3. Brewer and Bullen, *Cal. Car. MSS.* 179, 180; Kildare, *Earls of Kildare*, I. 57, 8; Gilbert, *Viceroys of Ireland*, 460.

4. Secret Instructions for Puebla to carry into England, Feb. 25, 1495.

5. André, *Vit. Hen. Sep.* 67—8; Henry's Instructions to Richmond King-at-Arms, Aug. 10, 1494; Fernando and Isabel to Puebla, July 20, 1495.

6. Isabel to Puebla, Aug. 8, 1490; Comines to the Signory, Oct. 3, 1494; Fernando and Isabel to Puebla, Jan. 30, Mar. 28, 1496; Fernando and Isabel to Henry, Jan. 30, 31, 1496.

7. Alexander to Puebla, April, 10, 1496; Fernando and Isabel to Puebla, April 14, 1496.

8. *Patent Rolls*, April 12, 1495, Mar. 18, 1496, Feb. 4, 1497.

CHAP. VII.—1. *Cronica del Gran Cardenal*, lib. II. c. 46.

2. *Europa Portuguesa*, pelo Faria y Sousa, II. 452; Graetz, *Geschichte der Juden*, VIII. 357, 386.

3. *Cronica del Gran Cardenal*, lib. II. c. 46.

4. Clemencin, *Elogio*, VI. 496; MCCCIX. to Alonzo de Compludo, Agent in London, Dec. 28, 1495; Jost, *Geschichte des Judenthums*, III. 113.

5. Spinola to Visconti, July 1 (?), Dec. 27, 1490; Isabel to Puebla, Aug. 18, 1496; Kayserling, *Geschichte der Juden in Portugal*, 120-39.

6. Santarem, *Quadro Elementar*, II. 3-6; Isabel to Puebla, Aug. 18, 1496.

CHAP. VIII.—1. Fray Tomas de Matienzo to Fernando and Isabel, Aug. 1498; Fray Andreas to Juana, Sep. 1, 1498.

2. Fléchier, *Histoire de Cardinal Ximenes*, 56; Castro, *Hist. Rel. Int.* 28.

3. *Capitulacion con Moros y Caballeros de Castilla*, Dec.

30, 1492; Conde, *Descripcion de España*, 4; Gayangos, *Hist. Moh. Dyn.* I. VIII.

4. Bergenroth, *Sup. Cal. Span. Pap.* 47, 48, 50, 405.
5. Fernando and Isabel to Puebla, July 20, Dec. 28, 1495.

CHAP. IX.—1. Fernando and Isabel to Puebla, Dec. 28, 1495; Contarini to the Signory, Aug. 22, 1495.
2. Contarini to the Signory, Aug. 22, 1495; Zurita, *Rey Hernando V.* lib. II. c. 5.
3. Isabel to Puebla, July 10, 1496; Fernando and Isabel to Puebla, July 6; Puebla to Fernando and Isabel, July 11.
4. Santarem, *Quadro Elementar*, II. 3; Mariana, *Hist. Esp.* II. 561; Graetz, *Geschichte der Juden*, VIII. 388-99; Lindo, *Hist. Jews*, 325-9.
5. Faria y Sousa, *Europa Portuguesa*, II. 494; Usque, *Tribulacoens de Ysrael*, 197-205; Kayserling, *Geschichte der Juden in Portugal*, 128.
6. Zurita, *Rey Hernando* V. 127; Ginsburg, *Cyc. Bibl. Lit.* III. 725.

SIXTH BOOK.

CHAP. I.—1. Bacon, *Works*, VI. 204; Kayserling, *Juden in Port.* 131; Guicciardini, *Storia d'Italia*, lib. III.; Zurita, *Anales*, V. lib. III. c. 6.
2. Puebla to Fernando and Isabel, July 17, 1498.
3. *Histoire du Cardinal Ximenes*, par Meyer Esprit Fléchier, 56-8; Puebla to Fernando and Isabel, July 17, 1498.
4. Treaty of Henry with Fernando and Isabel, Oct. 1, 1496; Puebla to Fernando and Isabel, June 13, 1496; Fernando and Isabel to Puebla, Dec. 28, 1495, June 21, July 11, 1496; Isabel to Puebla, Aug. 18, 1496.
5. Treaty of Henry with the Pope, the Emperor, Fernando and Isabel of Spain, and the Dukes of Venice and Milan, July 18, Sep. 23, 1496.
6. Fernando and Isabel to Puebla, January 30, 1496; Fernando and Isabel to Puebla, April 14, 1496; Alexan-

der VI. to Puebla, April 10, 1496; Maximilian to Puebla, April 18, 1496; Recontract of the Holy League, on the accession to it of Henry VII. July 18, 1496.

CHAP. II.—1. Burton, *Hist. Scotland*, III. 187; Gairdner, *Letters and Papers*, Ap. B. XVI.; *Mem. Hen. Sev.* 70.

2. *History of Scotland*, by John Pinkerton (London, 1797), II. 26-7; Gairdner, *Letters and Papers*, II. 73; André, *Vit. Hen. Sep.* 70; Richard, Duke of York, to Lady Catharine Gordon, Berg. *Sp. Cal.* I. 78.

3. Harl. MSS. 283, fo. 123 b. printed in Bacon's *Works*, VI. 252; Pinkerton, *Hist. Scot.* II. 29-30; *Archæologia*, XXVII. 181; *Fast. Eccl. Angl.* I. 142, 555, III. 292.

4. *Original Letters*, edited by Sir Henry Ellis, First Series, I. 22, 25; Tytler, *Hist. of Scotland*, III. 262-4; Pinkerton, *Hist. Scot.* II. 26-31; Isabel to Puebla, August 14, 1496.

5. Fernando and Isabel to Puebla, April 27, June 21, 1496; Isabel to Puebla, 14 August, 1496; Bacon's *Hist. of Hen. VII. Works*, VI. 1845; Hen. VII. to Fernando and Isabel, 18 Dec. 1500; Ayala to Fernando and Isabel, 14 July, 1498; Sub-Prior of Santa Cruz to Fernando and Isabel, July 18, 1498.

6. Bergenroth, *Cal. Sp. Pap.* I. 26; Isabel to Puebla, August 18, 1496.

7. Ayala to Fernando and Isabel, July 25, 1498; Tytler, *History of Scotland*, II. 263; Bergenroth, *Cal. Sp. Pap.* I. 26.

CHAP. III.—1. Isabel to Puebla, Aug. 18, 1496; Pinkerton, *Hist. Scot.* II. 37; Burton, *Hist. Scot.* III. 212-18; Tytler, *Hist. Scot.* II. 270.

2. Fernando and Isabel to Puebla, April 14, 26, 27, June 13, 21, July 11, Aug. 18, 1496; Isabel to Puebla, Aug. 25, 1496, Jan. 10, 1497; Fernando and Isabel to Londoño and Sub-Prior of Santa Cruz, Mar. 7, 1498; Hall, *Henry the Seventh*, XLV.

3. Bacon, *Hist. Hen. Sev. Works*, VI. 185; Rymer, *Fœdera*, XII. 572; *Mem. Hen. Sev.* 400; Fernando and Isabel to Londoño, Mar. 7, April 7, 1498.

4. Instructions to Bishop Fox, July 5, 1497; Puebla to Fernando and Isabel, Jan. 11, 1500.

5. Raimondo to Sforza, Sep. 8, 1497. (Venetian Transcripts, vol. XIV. 127.) Raimondo writes:—"Illustrissimo et excellentissimo Segnor mio. In multe cose cognosco questo principe essere sapientissimo ma sopra tutto per che sua Maesta intende benissimo le cose de Italia, et ha particulare aviso de ogni occorrentia et ditta Maesta intende le conditione de la vostra persona et del vostro stato non meno che lo Re Christianissimo et quando ditto Re passo in Italia li mando apresso uno suo Heraldo chiamato Richimondo homo savio chi ha veduto ogni cosa fin a la tornata poi li mercanti non cessano mai de avisare maxime fiorentini. Ultra de questo soa Maesta ha in Roma homini notabili como e messer Zoane Zilio Luchese et messer Adriano chierico de camera beneficiati et arrichiti da ditta Maesta per modo che non li havemo ditto cosa nova et anche li cortesani intendeno multo de le cose nostre per modo che me pare de essere in Roma. Unde io estimo sara bene fatto quando se vora avisare alcuna cosa overo notificarla piu distinctamente che li altri overo avisarla primo che li altri. In cio servira bene la scarsella de Genoa ma piu li mercanti fiorentini chi siano confidenti per che le cose loro passano per francia senza impedimento et se fa pocha cercata. E stata a proposito la congratulatione de la victoria regia scritta a XVII. de julio ma era pur tardetta et gia sono due victorie la prima contra Cornualiesi quali sotto uno ferraro se posseno in arme circa X^m dicendo non volevano paghare el subsidio laltra contra el Serenissimo Re de Scotia el quale se levato de campo non multo gloriosamente per non parlare cum manco modestia de quello fa questo Re sapientissimo. Et cosa che sua Maesta non me ha ditto quello giovene chi vorebe essere reputato filiolo del Re Eduardo e fugito incognito et la molie se dice essere presonera per modo che io reputo questo giovene ditto pirichino essere andato in fumo et stabilito el Regno ancora per lo successore che piaccia a dio cosi sia per che la virtu soa lo merita parlo del Illustrissimo principe. Et Vostra Excellentia po securamente congratularsi cum quelli Serenis-

simi Reali de Spagna de cosi prestante genero. Et tanto piu se potera iudicare stabilito se succede el matrimonio de Spagna cum ditto Serenissimo Re de Scotia che sono avisato se pratica. Et uno oratore hispano e presso ditto Re ma quando bene mancasse tale matrimonio questo regno e firmissimo primo per la sapientia de la quale ogniuno teme poi per le richeze che sono informato ha più de sei milioni d'oro et dicessi che ogni anno repone piu de cinquecento milia ducati che e facile cosa per che la intrata è grande viva non in scriptis, et non spende nulla. El guarda due o tre forteze fora del costume de li predecessori chi non guardavano alcuna del resto niente ne ordenanza ne altro. Estimo el non habia cento persone de guarda quantunche al presente habiti in loco foresto non munito. Tra le altre cose el sa bene intertenere ciascuno lo monstro avanti che io venessi in questo regno che volendo li oratori francesi andare in Scotia sotto nome de interpositione a la pace li festegio mirabilmente et li presento et li mando a casa senza vedere Scotia et hora manda uno suo camerero in francia. Perho è multo da laudare la Santita de nostro Signore quale lo ama cordialmente et lo favorisce in ogni cosa possibile fortificando questo regno de censure ecclesiastice per modo che in ogni tempo tutti li suoi rebelli sono excomunicati et la forza de questa censura hora e sentita da cornualiesi li quali sono in questo travalio che ciascuno chi mangia del grano recolto da poi la rebellione et chi beve de la cervosa fatta del recolto de questo anno more como se mangiasse veneno et de questo e publica fama che pare questo Re sia in tutela de dio eterno.

"Como scrissi de Anversa loratore cesareo non è venuto et meno lo pontificio solo se li ritrova lo hispano homo al parere mio dasai et dal quale mi pare essere bene visto che forsi ne e stata bona causa lhonorevolissimo parlare che io feci de quelli Serenissimi Reali in lo primo congresso. Loratore Napolitano se parte che me dispiace asai per che me haveria dato grande lume in ogni cosa et gia lha fatto de quanto ha potuto. Et per che el passara de qua Vostra Excellentia se potera informare da lui de multe cose et lo recomando a Vostra Illustrissima Signoria. Quam deus ad multos annos felicissimam conservet.

"Londonii VIII Septembris 1497.
Excellentie Vestre
       "Humilimus Servus Raimundus.
"Illustrissimo ac Excellentissimo Principi et domino meo colendissimo domino duci Mediolani, etc."

6. Raimondo to Sforza, Sep. 8, 1497; Tytler, *Hist. Scot.* II. 264.

CHAP. IV.—1. Bontius to Max, Nov. 6, 1496; Fernando and Isabel to Puebla, Jan. 10, Mar. 28, 1497.

2. *Privy Purse Expenses of Elizabeth of York*, XXI. XXII.; André, *Vit. Hen. Sep.* 65; Gilbert, *Viceroys of Ireland*, 427; *Annals of the Four Masters*, 306.

3. *Rot. Parl.* VI. 240; *Annals of the Four Masters*, 306; *Notes relative to the early History of the Town and Port of Hull*, by Charles Frost (London, 1827), 31; *Fast. Eccl. Angl.* II. 445, III. 143; Rymer, *Fœdera*, XII. 236, 250.

4. *Patent Rolls*, Mar. 11, 1486; André, *Vit. Hen. Sep.* 50-2; *Les Douze Triomphes de Henry Sept*, in Gairdner, *Mem. Hen. Sep.* 139; Frost, *Notes on Hull*, 31.

5. Napier, *Historical Notes of the Parishes of Swyncomb and Ewelme*, 162-9.

6. Raimondo to Sforza, Sep. 8, 1497; Halliwell, *Letters of the Kings of England*, I. 174; Gilbert, *Viceroys of Ireland*, 462; Brewer and Bullen, *Cal. Car. MSS.* 472; Anstiss, *Order of the Garter*, II. 215; Kildare, *Earls of Kildare*, I. 59, 60.

CHAP V.—1. *Patent Rolls*, June 20, 1497; Brewer and Bullen, *Cal. Car. MSS.* 472; Trevisano to the Signory, Sep. 17, 1497.

2. Henry to Puebla, Oct. 23, 1497; Halliwell, *Letters of the Kings of England*, I. 175-9; Hall, *Henry the Seventh*, XLI.

3. Trevisano to the Signory, Sep. 17, 1497; *News from England*, in Sanuto's *Diaries*, Nov. 6, 29, Dec. 31, 1497; Brewer and Bullen, *Cal. Car. MSS.* 468.

4. Raimondo to Sforza, Sep. 8, 1497; *Fœdera*, XII. 672-78; André, *Vit. Hen. Sep.* 72-3; Brewer and Bullen, *Cal. Car. MSS.* 469.

5. Scotch Treasurer's Accounts in Gairdner's *Letters and Papers*, App. B. XVI; Trevisano to the Signory, Nov. 29, 1497.

6. Puebla to Fernando and Isabel, June, July 17, 1498; Raimondo to Sforza, June 1, 1499.

7. Puebla to Fernando and Isabel, Jan. 18, 1500; *Statutes of the Realm*, II. 685; Bacon, *Works*, VI. 204.

CHAP. VI.—1. *Opus Epist. Pet. Mart.* Ep. 176; Mariana, *Hist. Esp.* II. 470-558; Madoz, *Diccionario de España*, IV. 167.

2. Santarem, *Quadro Elementar*, II. 1498; Zurita, *Rey Hernando V.* 561.

3. Faria y Sousa, *Europa Portuguesa*, II. 504-7.

4. Bergenroth, *Sup. Sp. Pap.* 47-50.

5. Isabel to Puebla, Aug. 18, 1496; Puebla to Fernando and Isabel, June 16, 1500; Santarem, *Quad. Elem.* II. 1499, 1500; Clemencin, *Elogio*, VI. 496.

6. Clemencin, *Elogio*, VI. lb. 15; *Op. Epist. Pet. Mart.* Ep. 215, 221; Giovio, *Vit. Mag. Gonsal.* 260; Mendoza, *Guerra de Granada*, 10-13.

7. Isabel to Puebla, April 8, May 7, 21, 29, July 5, 1501, Isabel to Henry, April 8, 1501; Almazan to Puebla, May 21, 1501; Henry to Cabra and Fonseca, Sep. 25, 1501.

8. Domengo Pisani to the Doge, Nov. 6, 1500; Arthur to Catharine, Oct. 5, 1499; Catharine's ratification at Granada, Dec. 20, 1500; Fabyan, *Chronicle*, 533; Gairdner, *Letters and Papers*, I. 129, 134, 233, 237; II. 377. Catharine's ratification runs:—

"20. Dec. 1500.

"*Littere originales scripte in pelle alba, quibus domina Catherina princeps Wallie.*

"Iterum ratificat matrimonium conclusum in capella manerii apud Bewdley per doctorem de la Puebla nomine suo et Arthurum principem Wallie in persona die xix mensis Maii anni MCCCCXCIX, nihilominus pro majore securitate jubet doctorem de iterum facere et concludere omnia et singula spectantia predictum matrimonium. Que fuerunt acta in civitate granate vicesimo die mensis Decembris anno a nativitate domini millesimo quingentesimo.

"LA PRINCESA DE GALES.
"Et ego Michael Perez D'Almazan."

CHAP. VII.—1. The Licentiate Alcarez to Isabel, Oct. 4, 1501; Gairdner, *Letters and Papers*, I. 126; Fabyan, *Chronicle*, 687.

2. Isabel to Puebla, Mar. 23, April 8, May 7, 1501; Isabel to Henry, April 8, 1501; Almazan to Puebla, May 21, 1501; Fernando and Isabel to Puebla, July 5, 1501; Henry to Fonseca and Cabra, Sep. 25, 1501.

3. Bergenroth, *Cal. Span. Pap.* I. 294; Grose, *Antiquarian Repertory*, II. 252; Alcarez to Isabel, Oct. 4, 1501.

4. Isabel to Estrada, Aug. 10, 1502; List of Catharine's household, Oct. 3, 1500.

5. Grose, *Ant. Rep.* II. 252; Henry to Fernando and Isabel, Dec. 18, 1500.

6. Henry to Catharine, Cott. MSS. Gal. B. II. f. 149; *Patent Rolls*, 2 Hen. VII. pt. III. 9.

7. Fernando and Isabel to Fuensalida, Bergenroth's *Cal. Sp. Pap.* I. 234; Fuensalida to Fernando and Isabel, June 29, 1500.

CHAP. VIII.—1. Puebla to Fernando and Isabel, June 16, Dec. 27, 1500; Fernando and Isabel to Fuensalida, *Cal. Sp. Pap.* I. 234.

2. Isabel to Puebla, Mar. 23, 1501; Grose, *Ant. Rep.* II. 25.

3. Grose, *Ant. Rep.* II. 253-4.

4. Grose, *Ant. Rep.* II. 254.

5. Arthur to Fernando and Isabel, Nov. 30, 1501; Grose, *Ant. Rep.* II. 255.

CHAP. IX.—1. Fabyan, *Chronicle*, 687; *Lelandi Collectanea* v. 354-5; Grose, *Antiq. Repert.* II. 256.

2. Fabyan, *Chron.* 687; Grose, *Ant. Rep.* II. 256.

3. Portrait of Arthur at Windsor Castle; *Patent Rolls*, June 12, 1488.

4. Tanner, *Notit. Monast.* 534; *Fast. Eccl. Angl.* III. 112; Grose, *Antiq. Repert.* II. 256.

5. Grose, *Antiq. Repert.* II. 259; Gairdner, *Letters and Papers*, I. 410.

6. *Patent Rolls*, 1 Hen. VII. pt. III. m. 4, 9, 16; Stow, *Annals*, 459; Anstiss, *Order of the Garter*, II. 217; Nott, *Works of the Earl of Surrey*, Int. v.; *Rot. Parl.* VI. 410; Collins, *Peerage of England*, I. 52, 79, 83.

7. Orridge, *Citizens of London and their Rulers*, 181; Nicolas, *Historic Peerage*, 367.

8. Grose, *Antiq. Repert.* II. 256-9; Hook, *Archbishops of Canterbury*, V. 490-515; Williams, *Lives of English Cardinals*, II. 190.

CHAP. X.—1. Grose, *Antiquarian Repertory*, II. 257; Old prints in the Gardner Collection; Northouck, *New History of London*, 107.

2. Grose, *Ant. Rep.* II. 319.

3. *The History of St. Paul's Cathedral*, by Sir William Dugdale, ed. Henry Ellis (London, 1818), 15, 20, 312; Butler, *Lives of Saints*, I. 544; *Lelandi Collectanea*, I. 22, 23.

4. Grose, *Ant. Rep.* II. 257.

5. *Fast. Eccl. Angl.* II. 298, III. 112; Dugdale, *Hist. Cath. St. Paul's*, 112; Hook, *Arch. Cant.* v. 519.

6. Grose, *Ant. Rep.* II. 258; Fabyan, *Chronicle*, 533.

7. Stow, *Annals*, 482; Hook, *Archbishops of Canterbury*, V. 520; Grose, *Ant. Rep.* II. 281-91; Hall, *Henry the Seventh*, LIV.

SEVENTH BOOK.

CHAP. I.—1. Henry to Fernando and Isabel, Nov. 28, 1501; Stow, *Annals*, 805-6; Hall, *Henry the Seventh*, fol. LIII. LIV.

2. Fernando and Isabel to Puebla, Jan. 6, 1502; Assignment of Catharine's dowry, Nov. 14, 1501; Stow, *Annals*, 807.

3. Herbert, *Life and Reign of Henry the Eighth*, 270; Grose, *Antiquarian Repertory*, II. 284-92; Hardyng, *Chronicle*, ed. Ellis, 584.

4. Fabyan, *Chronicle*, 687; Grose, *Ant. Rep.* II. 292, 318; Hall, *Henry the Seventh*, fol. LIV. LV.

5. Granger, *Biographical History of England*, I. 81; Kennedy, *Description of Wilton House*, 42; Laing, *Memoirs of William Dunbar*, 20; Green, *Princesses of England*, IV. 61; Grose, *Ant. Rep.* II. 291.

6. Arthur to Fernando and Isabel, Nov. 30; Henry to Fernando and Isabel, Nov. 28, 1501; Fernando and Isabel to Puebla, April 15, 1502. Arthur writes:—

Serenissimi ac potentissimi principes et domini mei, etc. Accepti superioribus diebus litteras Vestrarum Majestatum credentiales quas Reverendissimus Dominus Archiepiscopus Sancti Jacobi in Compostella et Illustris comes de Cabra nec non et episcopus Majoricarum, vestri oratores mihi reddiderunt, intellexique ex illis quemadmodum. Vestre Majestates per ipsos suos oratores Illustrissimam principem Dominam Chaterinam filiam suam uxorem meam charissimam tamdiu a me expectatam ad me misissent rogarentque idcirco quatenus eandem dominam principem benigne et humaniter vellem suscipere ac favorabiliter in cunctis tractare, Serenissimi domini mei, persuadere sibi tuto possunt Vestre Serenitates, me tam libenter ipsam meam dilectissimam conjugem vidisse ut nusquam majus aliquod gaudium meminerim me sensisse, itaque mihi desideratam faciem placuisse, ut nulla in toto orbe mihi magis satisfacere potuisset, moribus denique suis usque adeo me contentum tenere mihique esse satisfactum, ut nihil magis optarem: quam ob rem immortales habeo gracias vestris Serenitatibus, quod tam decoram tamque prestantem et modestam consortem mihi dederint; polliceorque bona fide non minus amicabiliter et favorabiliter esse me illam tracturum quam ego ipse tractari velim, et sicuti thori mei consors est facta, ita quoque et mee omnis felicitatis ac successus gaudiique et letitie particeps sit futura ita ut Vestre Majestates perpetuo se tenere contentas possint quod mihi fuerit desponsata, et ipsa quoque jucundissima sit perpetuo futura, quod me talem sibi maritum fuerit sortita. Restat igitur ut Vestre Majestates feliciter valeant et mihi semper, quacunque in re illis obsequi valeam, libere mandent, quoniam omni meo studio et cura semper enitar ut illis in omnibus morem geram.

Ex oppido de Richemonte die XXX Novembris, MCCCCCI.
ARTHURUS PRINCEPS WALLIE, filius vester deditissimus.

7. Ayala to Isabel, Berg. *Sup. Sp. Pap.* 2, 9. Herbert, *Life and Reign*, 270-3.

CHAP. II.—1. Powel, *History of Cambria*, 391; Brewer, *Calendar of State Papers (Henry VIII.)*, I. 88; Grose, *Antiquarian Repertory*, II. 319; Churton, *Life of Smyth;* Anstiss, *Register of the Order of the Garter*, II. 237; *Documents connected with the History of Ludlow and the Lords Marches*, by the Hon. R. H. Clive (London, 1841), 153.

2. Ayala to Isabel, Berg. *Sup. Sp. Pap.* 2; Marriage Treaty, Oct. 1, 1496.

3. Londoño and Matienzo to Fernando and Isabel, July 18, 1498; Breton to Londoño and Matienzo, July 18, 1498.

4. Matienzo to Fernando and Isabel, July 18, 1498; Spanish merchants to Londoño and Matienzo, July 18, 1498; Henry to Fernando and Isabel, Feb. 3, 1498; Jan. 27, 1499.

5. Ayala to Isabel, *Sup. Sp. Pap.* 2.

6. Bergenroth, *Sup. Sp. Pap.* 2, 3.

CHAP. III.—1. Bergenroth, *Sup. Sp. Pap.* 2, 3. Of the many letters which must have passed between the courts at this period only three or four have been left at Simancas.

2. Clive, *Doc. Hist. Lud.* 19; Anstiss, *Register of the Order of the Garter*, II. 237; Brewer, *Calendar of State Papers (Henry VIII.)*, I. 88; *Fast. Eccl. Angl.* III. 468.

3. Bergenroth, *Sup. Sp. Pap.* 4-5.

4. *Sup. Sp. Pap.* 6-9.

5. Grose, *Antiquarian Repertory*, II. 319, 20; *Sup. Sp.*

Pap. 9, 11; Tiraboschi, *Storia della Literatura Italiana* VI. 1446.
  6. *Biog. Univ.* XVII. 165; Bergenroth, *Sup. Sp. Pap.* 12.
  7. Fernando and Isabel to Puebla, Jan. 6, 1502; *Antiq. Rep.* II. 320; Hardyng, *Chronicle*, 584.

    CHAP. IV.—1. Cott. Mss. Vit. A. XVI. f. 198; *A Book of Scottish Pasquils* (Edin. 1868), Int. VIII. Ap. 418-22; Orridge, *London Citizens*, 122, 224; Mackenzie, *Lives of the most Eminent Writers of the Scots Nation*, II. 601.
  2. Ayala to Fernando and Isabel, July 25, 1496; Brown, *Calendar of Venetian Papers*, I. LIV.
  3. Ayala to Fernando and Isabel, July 25, 1496; Chalmers, *Caledonia*, b. II.; Sinclair, *Analysis of the Statistical Account of Scotland*, 71-107.
  4. *Chronicles of the Picts, Chronicles of the Scots, and other Early Memorials of Scottish History*, edited by W. F. Skene, Pref. LXXVIII. CXXII.; Buchanan, *Rerum Scoticarum Historia*, lib. VIII. 219; Sinclair, *Anal. Stat. Scot.* 14-18; Chalmers, *Caledonia*, b. II. III. IV.
  5. Scott, *Border Antiquities of England and Scotland*, App. VI.; Ridpath, *Border History of England and Scotland*, 1848.
  6. Ayala to Fernando and Isabel, July 25, 1496; Gibson, *History of Glasgow*, 74; Pinkerton, *History of Scotland*, I. 152.
  7. Billings, *Baronial and Ecclesiastical Antiquities of Scotland*, 1845-52; Mackenzie, *Writers of Scots Nation*, II. 144, 295, 376, 557; Laing, *Mem. of Dunbar*, prefixed to Dunbar's *Poems*, 20.

    CHAP. V.—1. Ayala to Fernando, July 25, 1496; Drummond, *History of Scotland from 1423 to 1542*, 183.
  2. Ayala to Fernando and Isabel, July 25, 1496; Tytler, *Hist. Scot.* II. 91, 185, 240; Ellis, *Original Letters*, First Series, I. 29.
  3. Ayala to Fernando and Isabel, July, 1496; Collins, *Peerage of England*, I. 68; Drummond, *Hist. Scot.* 229-33.
  4. Ayala to Fernando and Isabel, July 25, 1496;

Tytler, *History of Scotland*, II. 246-269; Douglas, *Peerage of Scotland*, I. 269; Drummond, *Hist. Scot.* 232.

5. Ayala to Fernando and Isabel, July 25, 1496; Douglas, *Peerage of Scotland*, I. 51, II. 361; Tytler, *Hist. Scot.* App. II. 394; Mackenzie, *Writers of Scots Nation*, II. 554; *New Statistical Account of Scotland*, X. 320.

6. Pitcairn, *Historical and Genealogical Account of the Kennedys*, 82, 83; Douglas, *Peerage of Scotland*, I. 328.

7. Drummond, *Hist. Scot.* 232-3; Tytler, *Hist. Scot.* App. II. 394.

CHAP. VI.—1. Stow, *Survey of London*, b. IV. c. 3; Fuller, *Holy War*, lib. v.; Hollar, *View of St. John of Clerkenwell*. Some copies of Dugdale's *Monasticon* have fine impressions of this view. There is a poor copy in *Londina Illustrata*, p. 48. The copy under my own eyes is that in the great collection of prints illustrating Old London, made by J. E. Gardner, Esq.

2. Cromwell, *History and Description of Clerkenwell*, 122, 130; Pinks, *History of Clerkenwell*, 197, 240; Hardy, *Patent Rolls in the Tower*, 159.

3. *Foedera*, v. pt. 4, 165, 7; Bacon, *Works*, VI. 216, 17.

4. Grafton, *Chronicle*, abrid. 136; Orridge, *Citizens of London*, 32, 224; Halliwell, *History of New Place*, 2, 3; Collins, *Peerage of England*, III. 348.

5. Norton, *Commentaries on the History and Constitution of the City of London* (London, 1869), b. I. c. 8; Orridge, *Citizens of London*, 222, 224; Dunbar's Poem, in *Cotton MSS.*, Vit. A. XVI. 198.

6. *Foedera*, v. pt. 4, 168; Tytler, *Hist. Scot.* II. 269; Green, *Princesses of England*, IV. 63, 4.

CHAP. VII.—1. Clive, *Documents connected with the History of Ludlow*, 1-18; *History and Antiquities of the Town of Ludlow* (Lud. 1822), 49, 60; Grose, *Antiquities of England and Wales*, III. art. Ludlow.

2. Grose, *Antiquarian Repertory*, II. 321; Herbert, *Henry the Eighth*, 270-3.

3. Henry to Fernando and Isabel, Feb. 20, 1502. This letter from Henry to Fernando and Isabel has been re-

moved from the State collection at Simancas. When and why the removal took place is matter of inference. Not long ago it was in the private cabinet of Isabel the Second, and was given by her as an autograph to Eugenie, then Empress of the French. A copy, certified by M. Teulet, is in the Record Office, Fetter Lane; the text is printed in *Court and Society*, I. 59.

4. Grose, *Ant. Rep.* II. 322; Clive, *Doc. Hist. Lud.* 19.
5. *Hist. Antiq. Ludlow*, 63; Clive, *Doc. Hist. Ludlow*, 20; *Antiq. Rep.* 322; Powell, *History of Cambria*, 392.
6. Grose, *Ant. Rep.* II. 322, 3.

CHAP. VIII.—1. Hollar's View of Greenwich, in the Gardner Collection; *Archaeologia*, II. XXV.; Lysons, *Environs of London*, I. 519.
2. Stow, *Annals*, 484.
3. Grose, *Antiquarian Repertory*, II. 322; Green, *Princesses of England*, IV. 506, V. 3.
4. Lelandi Collectanea, V. 372.
5. Lel. Coll. V. 372; *Privy Purse Exp. Eliz. York*, Int. LXI.
6. Lel. Coll. V. 373.

EIGHTH BOOK.

CHAP. I.—1. Carvajal, *Documentos Ineditos*, XVIII. 304; Powers given to Estrada, May 10, 1502; Gamero, *Historia de Toledo*, lib. II. c. 6; Grose, *Antiq. Rep.* II. 319.
2. Fernando and Isabel to Estrada, May 10, 1502; Giannone, *Istoria di Napoli*, lib. XXIX. c. 4; Martin, *Hist. de France*, VIII. 412-5.
3. Fernando and Isabel to Puebla, May 10, 1502.
4. *Documents Originaux de l'Histoire de France*, 313, 314; *Mémoires de Comines*, lib. VIII. c. 23; Baudier, *Histoire de l'Administration du Cardinal d'Amboise*, 74; Guicciardini, *Storia d'Italia*, lib. V. c. 1, 2, 3; Mariana, *Historia de España*, lib. XXVII. c. 16; Bernaldez, *Reyes Catolicos*, c. 166.

5. Instructions for Estrada, May 10, 1502.
6. Instructions for Estrada, May 10, 1502. The first set of instructions for Estrada read:—

Ferdinandus et Elizabeth dei gratia rex et regina Castelle, etc. Confidentes admodum de fide legalitate et animi integritate vestri Ferdinandi Duque de Estrada magistri Aule, consiliarii et oratoris nostri, tenore presentis de nostra certa scientia deliberate et consulto eis omnibus melioribus via, modo et forma quibus de jure et alias possumus et valemus, facimus, constituimus, creamus et ordinamus nostrum verum certum legitimum et indubitatum procuratorem. oratorem et nuntium specialem et ad infra scripta generalem, ita tamen quod specialitas generalitati non deroget, nec e contra, vos eundem Ferdinandum Duque de Estrada, videlicet ut pro nobis et nomine nostro ac nomine Illustrissime Catherine principis Wallie infantis Castelle et Aragonum filie nostre dilectissime possitis petere, recipere, recuperare a serenissimo Enrico rege Anglie fratre nostro dilectissimo illa centum millia scuta auri justi et recti ponderis ac valoris, que eidem Serenissimo regi Anglie in pecunia numerata realiter et cum effectu solvimus isque a nobis recepisse confessus est in solutionem medietatis dotis per nos promisse cum prefata illustrissima principe et infante Catherina filia nostra in contractu per utrasque partes inito et firmato super matrimonio, quod concordatum et contractum fuerat inter illustrissimum quondam Arthurum principem Wallie ejusdem serenissimi regis Anglie fratris nostri dilectissimi primogenitum et heredem bone memorie et eandem illustrissimam Catherinam principem et infantem filiam nostram: possitisque, cum predicta centum millia escuta auri recuperaveritis, de illorum receptione nomine nostro et ejusdem illustrissime principis et infantis filie nostre et pro nobis facere, concedere. firmare et tradere eidem serenissimo regi Anglie fratri nostro quascumque apocas, albarana, definiciones et alias legitimas cautelas: et nihilominus possitis pro nobis et nomine nostro et dicte principis et infantis filie nostre requirere et procurare apud eundem serenissimum regem Anglie fratrem nostrum, quod tertia pars reddituum principatus Wallie, ducatus Cornubie et comitatus Castrie, que virtute prefati contractus matrimonialis eidem assignari et tradi debet pro sustentatione sui status, assignetur et detur eidem in bonis villis et locis ubi ipsa dictam tertiam partem reddituum seu ejus justum valorem anno quolibet libere et absque impedimento aliquo colligere et levare possit: Si res ista hactenus expedita non fuerit, preterea possitis pro nobis et nomine nostro requirere et instare ac rogare eundem Serenissimum regem Anglie fratrem nostrum, omne id totum et quidquid conveniat pro reditu in Hispaniam ad eos prefate illustrissime principis et infantis filie nostre onusque illam recipiendi et ad nos deferendi una cum aliis personis quas ad eam comitandam deputavimus per vos declarandis acceptare et accipere: et inde nomine nostro eidem serenissimo regi Anglie fratri nostro concedere facere et tradere quamcunque exonerationem necessariam et opportunam ac per eundem Serenissimum regem petitam; et generaliter possitis in predictis et circa ea nomine nostro et pro nobis omnia alia et singula facere, procurare et concedere et firmare que necessaria fuerint quomodolibet et opportuna et que nos facere possimus si in premissis personaliter adessemus, etiam si talia sint que ad ea conficiendum mandatum exigant magis speciale quam presentibus est expressum, dantes et concedentes vobis predicto oratori et procuratori nostro plenum posse et generale mandatum ad premissa omnia et singula faciendum cum libera et generali administratione, promittentes eidem serenissimo regi Anglie fratri nostro nos habere ratum gratum validum atque firmum omne id totum, et quidquid per vos predictum oratorem et procuratorem nostrum in predictis et quolibet predictorum nomine nostro fuerit factum et firmatum et illud nullo unquam tempore revocare: In cujus rei testimonium presentes fieri jussimus manibus nostris signatas sigilloque nostro in pendenti munitas.

Datum in civitate Toleti die decimo mensis Maii anno a nativitate domini millesimo quingentesimo secundo.

Yo el Rey.   Yo el Reyna.

The second, and more important, set of instructions, read:—

Ferdinandus et Helizabeth dei gratia rex et regina Castelle, Legionis, etc. Quoniam pro majori observantia et securitate confederationis et amicitia que est inter nos et Serenissimum Enricum regem Anglie fratrem nostrum dilectissimum et pro augmento affinitatis nostre fuit tractatum, quod Illustrissima Catherina princeps Wallie ac infans Castelle et Aragonum filia nostra charissima contrahat matrimonium cum Illustrissimo Enrico principe Wallie filio legitimo et herede ejusdem Serenissimi regis Anglie fratris nostri, et quia mens et voluntas nostra est, si eidem Serenissimo regi ita placuerit, quod predictum matrimonium, deo annuente, fiat et concludatur, propterea confidentes admodum de fide, prudentia, legalitate et animi integritate vestri Ferdinandi Duque de Strada magistri Aule et consiliarii nostri, tenore presentiarum de nostra certa scientia deliberate et consulte eis omnibus melioribus via modo et forma quibus de jure et alias possumus et valemus, facimus constituimus, etc. nostrum verum certum legitimum et indubitatum procuratorem, oratorem, etc. specialem et ad infra scripta generalem, ita tamen quod specialitas generalitati non deroget nec e contra, vos eundem Ferdinandum Duque de Strada, videlicet ut pro nobis et nomine nostro possitis tractare et concordare et firmare cum dicto Serenissimo rege Anglie fratre nostro sponsalia et matrimonium predicte illustrissime principis et infantis Catherine filie nostre charissime cum dicto illustrissimo principe Wallie Enrico filio legitimo et herede dicti Serenissimi regis Anglie fratris nostri et promittere quod nos faciemus et curabimus dabimusque operam cum effectu quod dicta illustrissima princeps et infans Catherina filia nostra predicta sponsalia et matrimonium faciet, concedet et contrahet per verba de presenti, matrimonium facientia juxta ordinem Sancte Romane ecclesie, cum dicto illustrissimo Enrico principe Wallie, filio legitimo et herede dicti Serenissimi regis Anglie fratris nostri, cum ipse ad legitimam pervenerit etatem ad illud faciendum, concedendum et contrahendum, et quod postea celebrabit et consumabit dictum

matrimonium cum dicto illustrissimo Enrico principe
Wallie prout et quemadmodum legitime vir et uxor facere
debent: possitisque nomine nostro et predicte principis
et infantis Catherine filie nostre petere et recipere simi-
lem promissionem et obligationem a dicto Serenissimo
rege Anglie fratre nostro pro se ipso et nomine predicti
Enrici principis Wallie ejus filii, videlicet quod cum ipse
princeps ad legitimam pervenerit etatem, ut prefertur,
faciet sponsalia et contrahet matrimonium per verba de
presenti juxta ordinem sacrosancte matris ecclesie Romane cum dicta illustrissima principe infante Catherina
filia nostra et consumabit et celebrabit cum ea dictum
matrimonium prout et quemadmodum legitimi vir et uxor
id facere debent: et possitis concedere et firmare quod
predicta fieri debeant et adimpleri modis formis tempo-
ribus et locis quibus vobis dicto oratori et procuratori
nostro bene visum fuerit, et prout ea vos concordabitis,
concedetis, capitulabitis et firmabitis: damus etiam et
potestatem et facultatem vobis prefato oratori et procuratori nostro ut possitis concordare et firmare cum dicto
Serenissimo rege Anglie fratre nostro dotem quam nos
dare teneamur cum dicta principe et infante Catherina
filia nostra tam in jocalibus atque lapidibus preciosis et
in argento et vestibus et ornamentis persone et domus
sue, quam in pecuniis, summam videlicet et quantitatem
que nobis bene visa fuerit et terminis et locis quibus
istam dare et solvere teneamur et conditiones, pacta et
conventiones que in solutione et restitutione ejusdem
dotis poni et concedi et firmari debent, et nihilominus
damus vobis potestatem et facultatem ut possitis petere
et concordare augmentum dotis et donationis propter
nuptias et cameram, que debent dari et assignari dicto
principi et infanti Catherine filie nostre pro sustentatione
sui status, et in quibus civitatibus, villis et locis et reddi-
tibus, prout vobis dicto oratori nostro bene visum fuerit:
et demum possitis facere et firmare omnia et singula que
pro expeditione et complemento dicti matrimonii necessaria, convenientia et opportuna vobis videbuntur, et de
predictis omnibus et singulis possitis concordare facere
et firmare nomine nostro cum prefato Serenissimo rege

Anglie fratre nostro, fierique facere petere et instare quecunque capitula et quoscunque tractatus cum illis pactis conditionibus etc. quibus volueritis, et generaliter omnia alia et singula facere et firmare, cujuscunque nature, qualitatis et importantie fuerint aut esse poterint, in predictis et circa ea que nos facere possemus si in premissis personaliter adessemus, etiam si talia sint que ad ea conficienda preceptum exigant magis speciale: Damus etiam et concedimus vobis dicto procuratori et oratori nostro plenum posse, quod possitis jurare in animas nostras quod tenebimus etc. omnia et singula que in predictis et circa ea nomine nostro concordabitis etc. possitisque simile juramentum petere et decipere ab eodem Serenissimo rege Anglie etc.; Pro quibus omnibus et singulis antedictis cum invidentibus, dependentibus etc. damus et concedimus vobis plenum posse cum libera et generali administratione; promittentes in fide et verbo nostro regiis prefato Serenissimo regi Anglie fratri nostro et obligamus nos tenere et adimplere etc. omnia et singula que in predictis et circa ea nomine nostro per vos dictum procuratorem et oratorem nostrum fuerint facta, concordata, jurata etc. eis modo et forma quibus vos ea concordabitis etc. et nullo unquam tempore revocare nec contra ea aut eorum aliquod facere vel venire aliquo tempore nec modo aliquo sub obligatione omnium bonorum nostrorum patrimonialium et fiscalium: In quorum testimonium presentem fieri jussimus manibus nostris signatam sigilloque nostro in pendenti munitam.

Datum in civitate Toleti die decimo mensis Maii anno a nativitate domini millesimo quingentesimo secundo.

7. Fernando and Isabel to Estrada, May 10, June 14, 1502.

CHAP. II. -1. Fernando and Isabel to Puebla, May 12, 1502.

2. Fernando and Isabel to Estrada, June 14, 1502. This important letter from Puebla has been removed from Simancas. When and why it was removed is matter of conjecture, taken in relation to the great controversies of after years. We know that Charles the Fifth had a col-

lection of Puebla's letters in his hands. See Edward Lee to Henry the Eighth, April 20, 1529.

3. Giustinian to Estrada, May 10, 1502; Fernando and Isabel to Estrada, June 14, 16, 1502.

4. Fernando and Isabel to Estrada, June 16, 1502; Gregorio di Casale to Henry the Eighth, Dec. 26, 1532.

5. Puebla to Isabel, in Bergenroth, *Cal. Sp. Papers*, I. 339.

6. Fernando and Isabel to Estrada, June 16, 1502; *Biog. Univ.* XVII. 165.

7. Fernando and Isabel to Estrada, June 28, 1502; Opinions of the Doctors of Salamanca, April 12, 1502.

8. Isabel to Estrada, July 12, Aug. 10, 1502, April 12, 1503; Bernaldez, *Reyes Catolicos*, c. 168.

CHAP. III.—1. My Note Book; Act of Marriage, May 19, 1499; Powel, *Hist. Camb.*, 392; *Lelandi Collectanea*, V. 373-8; Murray, *Handbook of Worcester Cathedral*, 212-3.

2. Bacon, *Works*, VI. 214. Not a word of the important correspondence between Catharine and her mother or between Elvira and her mistress at this period is to be found at Simancas.

3. Old Prints in the Gardner Collection; Harris, *Historic Peerage*, 576, 590; Edwards, *Life of Raleigh*, II. 262.

4. Ducarel, *History of Croydon*, 40-70; Lysons, *Environs of London, Surrey*, I. part I. 126-8; Malcolm, *Manners and Customs of London*, 453; Hook, *Archbishops of Canterbury*, V. 516; *Journal of the Archæological Institute*, XVIII. 267; Duck, *Life of Chichele*, 174.

5. Fabyan, *Chronicle*, 688; Herbert, *Life and Reign of Henry the Eighth*, 2.

6. Gairdner, *Letters and Papers*, I. XLI.; Fabyan, *Chronicle*, 688.

CHAP. IV.—1. Fernando and Isabel to Puebla, May 21, 1502; *Documents Originaux de France*, 314, 315; *Lettres des Rois, Collections de Documents Inédits sur l'Histoire de France*, II. 511; Seysell, *Histoire de Louis XII.*, 205-18; Baudier, *Admin. du Cond. d'Amboise*, 21, 23, 26, 61; Novaes, *Pontefici da San Pietro*, VI. 94.

2. Isabel to Estrada, Aug. 12, 1502.
3. Fernando and Isabel to Puebla, June 15, Aug. 10, 1502; Isabel to Estrada, Aug. 10, 1502; Fernando and Isabel to Estrada, Dec. 13, 1502. Estrada's confidential correspondence has been removed from Simancas. It is only from the King and Queen's replies that we gather the particulars here set forth.
4. Fernando and Isabel to Estrada, June 14, 1502; Isabel to Puebla, Aug. 10, 1502; *Biog. Univ.* XVII. 165.
5. Fernando and Isabel to Estrada, June 14, 1502; Isabel to Estrada, Aug. 10, 1502; Tiraboschi, *Storia della Literatura Italiana*, VI. 1446-7.
6. Indorsement on Fernando's letter, June 14, 1502; Quirini to the Signory, Mar. 31, 1505; Herbert, *Life and Reign of Henry VIII.*
7. Guicciardini, *Storia d'Italia*, lib. V. c. 3, 4; Herbert, *Life and Reign of Henry VIII.*, 7; Hook, *Archbishops of Canterbury*, new series, I. 195; *Fast. Eccl. Angl.* I. 41, 171, 11-52.

CHAP. V.—1. Carvajal, *Documentos ineditos*, XVIII. 302-5; Guicciardini, *Storia d'Italia*, lib. V. c. 3, 4; Novaes, *Pontefici da San Pietro*, VI. 95-116; Sismondi, *Hist. Rep. Ital.* VII. 85, 92; Manrique, *Regimiento de Principes*, in *Cancionero General* 1520. Readers who wish to judge how much of liberal thought and spiritual independence survived in Spain, notwithstanding all the efforts of Isabel's inquisitors, should study the *Reformistas Antiguos Españoles*, edited by Don Luis de Usos y Rios, 20 volumes; particularly, '*Artes de la Inquisición Española*, by Montes; *Alfabeto Christiano*, and *Ziento y diez Consideraziones*, by Valdez; and *Breve Sumario de Induljenzias*, by Perez. For a list of the prohibited books published in Spain in the century of Isabel's death, see *History of Religious Intolerance in Spain*, by Adolfo de Castro, Ap. 1.
2. Isabel to Estrada, July 12, 1502. The important letter of Elvira referred to by Isabel has been removed from Simancas.
3. Isabel to Estrada, July 12, 1502.
4. Novaes, *Pontefici da San Pietro*, VI. 109; Martire,

De Legatione Babylonicæ, 76, et seq.; Garibay, *Compendio*, II. lib. XIX. c. 12; Guicciardini, *Storia d'Italia*, lib. V. c. 3.
  5. Isabel to Estrada, July 12, 1502.
  6. Isabel to Estrada, July 12, 1502.

  CHAP. VI.—1. Fernando and Isabel to Puebla, July 18, 1502; Isabel to Puebla, Aug. 10, 1502; Gamero, *Historia de Toledo*, lib. II. c. 5.
  2. Isabel to Puebla, Aug. 10, 1502.
  3. Giovio, *Vita Magni Gonsalvi*, lib. II. 203-9; Guicciardini, *Storia d'Italia*, lib. V. c. 3, 4; Novaes, *Pontefici da San Pietro*, VI. 110; Martin, *Histoire de France*, VIII. 414; Sismondi, *Hist. Rep. Ital.* VII. 83-98; Hammer, *Histoire de l'Empire Ottoman*, IV. 66, 75.
  4. Isabel to Estrada, Aug. 10, 1502.
  5. Isabel to Estrada, Aug. 10, 1502.
  6. Isabel to Estrada, Aug. 10, 1502.

  CHAP. VII.—1. Fernando to Estrada, Sep. 1, 1502; Isabel to Estrada, Aug. 21, 25, 1502; Giovio, *Vit. Mag. Gonsal.* lib. II. 209; Guicciardini, *Storia d'Italia*, lib. V. c. 4, 5; Sismondi, *Hist. Rep. Ital.* VII. 93.
  2. Bernaldez, *Reyes Catolicos*, c. 165; Mendoza, *Guerra de Granada*, 13; Martire, *De Legatione Babylonicæ*, 81; Ballaguer, *Historia de Cataluña*, lib. IX. c. 1.
  3. Isabel to Puebla, Sep. 30, 1502; Fernando to Estrada, Sep. 1, 1502; Fernando and Isabel to Rojas, Nov. 17, 1502.
  4. Fernando and Isabel to Estrada, Dec. 13, 1502; Draft of Articles, Sep. 24, 1502, in *Cott. MSS. Vesp.* c. XII. 218.
  5. Fernando and Isabel to Estrada, Dec. 13, 1502.
  6. Fernando and Isabel to Estrada, Dec. 13, 1502.

NINTH BOOK.

  CHAP. I—1. *Privy Purse Expenses of Eliz. of York*, 3-70; Lambarde, *Perambulations of Kent*, 386; *Rot. Parl.* VI. 270.

2. *Lelandi Collectanea*, V. 375-8; Hall, *Henry the Seventh*, LV.

3. Brayley, *Westminster Abbey*, II. 79; *Privy Purse Expenses of Henry the Seventh*, in *Excerpta Historica*, 85; *Privy Purse Exp. Eliz. York*, 3, 29; Gough, *Sepulchral Monuments*, II. p. 3, 327.

4. Dart, *Westmonasterium*, 1, 3, 9, 14, 20, 26, 32; Butler, *Lives of Saints*, II. 343-55; Stanley, *Mem. West. Abb.* 156-9.

5. Powel, *History of Cambria*, 390; Lynch, *Law and Usage of the Prescriptive Baronies of Ireland*, 38; Stanley, *Mem. West. Abbey*, 160.

CHAP. II.—1. Tighe, *Annals of Windsor*, I. 429.

2. Pinks, *History of Clerkenwell*, 217; Dart, *Abbots of West.* II. XXXIV.; Henry the Seventh's Will in Record Office, Richmond, Mar. 31, 1509; Old prints in the Gardner Collection.

3. *History of the Ancient Savoy Palace*, by J. Bruce, 5, 6; Nicolas, *Historic Peerage*, 395; *Cott. MSS. Cleop.* V. c. 1; Collins, *Life of Edward the Black Prince*, 1740.

4. Hardy, *Close Rolls*, Pref. XXX.; Furnival, *Ballads from Manuscripts*, I. Pt. I. 158-62; Howel, *Londinopolis*, 356; Newton, *London in the Olden Time*, 15, 78, 83, 88; Nelson, *History of the Parish of St. Mary, Islington*, 192; Old Prints in the Gardner Collection.

5. Morley, *Memoirs of Bartholomew Fair*, 2-9; Doran, *History of Court Fools*, 102-6; Dugdale, *Baronage of England*, II. 81; *Rot. Parl.* V. 571, 606; Stow, *Survey of London*, 304; Ducarel, *History of the Hospital of St. Catharine*, 7-20; Newton, *London in the Olden Time*, 9; Old Plans and Prints in the Gardner Collection.

6. Institutiones et Statuta Hospitalis de Savoy, *Cott. MSS. Cleop.* V. art. 1; Notes touching the Foundation and Endowments of the Savoy Hospital, *Harl. MSS.* 604, f. 22.

CHAP. III.—1. Guicciardini, *Storia d'Italia*, lib. V. c. 4, 5; Giovio, *Vita. Mag. Gonsal.* lib. II. 205; Sismondi, *Hist. Rep. Ital.* VII. 86; *Mémoires de Bayard*, par le Loyal Serviteur, c. XXIII.

2. Gairdner, *Letters and Papers*, I, 141; Fabyan, *Chronicle*, 688; *Fœdera*, V. 26.

3. Puebla to Fernando and Isabel, June 16, 1500; Doge and Senate to Trevisano and others, Feb. 17, 1501; Fernando and Isabel to Puebla, April 29, 1503; Juana to Fuensalida, May 11, 1509; Fernando to Fuensalida, May 14, 1509; *Chronicle of Calais*, 5.

4. *Privy Purse Expenses of Elizabeth of York*, XCI; Green, *Lives of the Princesses of England*, V. 144; Fabyan, *Chronicle*, 688.

5. André, *Cott. MSS.* Dom. A. XVIII.; Mocenigo to the Signory, Mar. 20, 1503; Isabel to Estrada, April 11, 12, 1503; Grose, *Antiq. Report*, IV. 654; *Privy Purse Expenses of Eliz. of York*, XCIII.

END OF VOL. II.

www.ingramcontent.com/pod-product-compliance
Lightning Source LLC
Chambersburg PA
CBHW020757230426

43666CB00007B/728